Captain *of* Innocence

Captain *of* Innocence

France & the Dreyfus Affair

Norman H. Finkelstein

illustrated with prints and photographs

G. P. PUTNAM'S SONS · New York

G. P. Putnam's Sons, a division of The Putnam & Grosset Book Group,
200 Madison Avenue, New York, NY 10016.
Published simultaneously in Canada.
Printed in the United States of America.

Book design by Joy Taylor

Library of Congress Cataloging-in-Publication Data

Finkelstein, Norman H.
    Captain of innocence : France and the Dreyfus affair / Norman H.
Finkelstein.
    p. cm.
    Includes bibliographical references.
    Summary: Surveys the life, multiple trials, imprisonment, and
eventual release of the Jewish French army officer accused of spying
for the Germans.
    1. Dreyfus, Alfred, 1859–1935—Juvenile literature.   2. France—
Politics and government—1870–1940—Juvenile literature.
    3. Antisemitism—France—History—19th century—Juvenile literature.
    4. Trials (Treason)—France—History—19th century—Juvenile
literature.   [1. Dreyfus, Alfred, 1859–1935.   2. Jews—Biography.
    3. Antisemitism—France—History—19th century.]   I. Title.
DC354.F56   1991
305.892′4049′09034—dc20
[92]
                                                              90-27845
                                                                   CIP
                                                                    AC

Photograph credits

Beth Hatefutsoth. The Nahum Goldmann Museum of the Jewish Diaspora,
Israel: pp. 17, 56, 68, 93, 112–113, 120.
The Central Archives for the History of the Jewish People, Israel: pp. 20, 98,
105, 109, 115.
The Library of Congress: pp. 82, 126, 136.
National Archives: pp. 29, 34–35, 38, 51, 60–61, 80, 95, 130.

ISBN 0-399-22243-X

10 9 8 7 6 5 4 3 2 1

First Impression

FOR

Rachel, Georges, and Lise

PARIS

Acknowledgments

Grateful acknowledgment is made to the following for permission to quote from copyrighted material.

George Braziller, Inc., for quotations from
The Affair: The Case of Alfred Dreyfus by Jean-Denis Bredin
Copyright © 1986 by George Braziller, Inc.

The Estate of Nicholas Halasz for quotations from
Captain Dreyfus by Nicholas Halasz
Published by Simon & Schuster
Copyright © 1955 by Nicholas Halasz

William Morrow and Company for quotations from
Prisoners of Honor—The Dreyfus Affair by David L. Lewis
Copyright © 1973 by David L. Lewis

Rutgers University Press for quotations from
The Dreyfus Case: A Documentary History by Louis L. Snyder
Copyright © 1973 by Rutgers University,
The State University of New Jersey

———————————

I am indebted to the following for their assistance during my research visits: Dr. Murray Tuchman, Librarian, and the staff of the Hebrew College Library, Brookline, Massachusetts. Ruth Porter, Director, Photo Archives, Beth Hatefutsoth, Tel Aviv University, Israel. Fabienne Sadan, Archivist, The Center for the History of the Jewish People, Hebrew University, Jerusalem, Israel. The staffs of: The Israel Museum, Jerusalem, the Bibliothèque Nationale, Paris, The Library of the Jewish Theological Seminary of America, New York, and the Houghton Library, Harvard University, Cambridge. I especially thank my wife, Rosalind, and my children, Jeffrey, Robert, and Risa, for their continuing support.

N.H.F.

Contents

Captain *of* Innocence

· ONE ·

Honor Denied

Long live France. Long live the army!
—*Alfred Dreyfus*

Death to the Jew! —*Response from the mob*

IF YOU stand in the center of Place Fontenoy on Paris's Left Bank and face the Eiffel Tower looming in the distance, the École Militaire is directly in front of you. Beyond the tall, black bars of a wrought-iron fence, its tops gleaming with gold paint, you can see the imposing dome of the famous War College's gray stone buildings. On a typical Saturday morning in January, the vast open courtyard in the foreground is deserted. Just outside the fence on Avenue de Lowendal, only an occasional passerby, bundled up against the cold, hurries silently past.

Early on January 5, 1895, another gray winter Saturday, the buildings, courtyard, and Eiffel Tower looked much the same as they do today. The stillness of the picture-postcard landscape was broken by the sight and sound of two distinct groups gathered on either side of the iron fence.

In the courtyard were five thousand soldiers representing

15

all army units in Paris. Carefully, they arranged themselves by companies squarely around the courtyard perimeter. In the center, astride a horse, was General Paul Darras, the officer in charge of the ceremony. Military music and sharply issued commands echoed off the walls of the École Militaire and reverberated in the square outside. There, a growing crowd of Parisians, numbering more than 20,000, jostled for the best viewing positions. They mingled quietly at first. No one smiled. They were not here to be amused. They came to savor revenge. A traitor was about to be deservedly humiliated.

The crime was high treason. The condemned officer had been found guilty of passing military secrets to France's archenemy, Germany.

As the college's clock struck nine, General Darras raised his sword and commanded, "Present arms!" His order was sharply repeated by the head of each company, and the assembled soldiers came rigidly to attention. The hushed crowd watched expectantly. From an entrance on the left, a small procession emerged, consisting of four sword-bearing soldiers led by an imposing sergeant of the Republican Guard. They surrounded a slight army captain, who marched along with a steady step, his body erect and head held high.

So silent had the crowds become that the clacking of the marching group's boots on the cobblestones was clearly heard. There he was, the traitor. All eyes focused on the captain. It was his degradation everyone was here to see.

When the small procession arrived in front of General Darras, still on horseback, the general dramatically drew his sword and exclaimed for all to hear, "Alfred Dreyfus, you are unworthy of carrying arms. In the name of the people of France, we degrade you."

To the shock of the assembled soldiers and the crowd outside, the captain suddenly cried out in an emotional voice: "Soldiers, they are degrading an innocent man. Soldiers, they are dishonoring an innocent man. Long live France! Long live the

The Degradation of Captain Dreyfus *by Frederick de Haenen, originally published in* L'Illustration *on January 12, 1895.*

army!" The pent-up anger of the crowd now exploded. "Death to the Jew!" they shouted.

The seven-foot-tall Sergeant Bouxin faced the captain. Looming like a giant over the much shorter officer, the sergeant dramatically began his assigned duty. With theatrical flourish he ripped the buttons, trouser stripes, and insignia from the captain's uniform. The torn items lay in a forlorn heap on the ground. He next received the officer's sword and broke it in two across his knee. With a bold sweep the sergeant flung the pieces onto the pile.

In the remains of his tattered uniform, the humiliated captain was then led in a quick-paced march around the courtyard past the precisely arranged rows of soldiers. While most soldiers maintained their military bearing, reporters noticed that some were overcome with the emotion of the moment as they watched a colleague endure a soldier's ultimate humiliation.

With his head still held high, the captain again shocked the crowd by crying over and over: "I am innocent! I am innocent! Long live France!" As his words floated over the gates of the courtyard, the intensity of the mob's howling only increased. "Death to the Jew! Death to the traitor!"

As the little procession moved past a group of journalists, the captain turned and shouted: "You must tell all of France that I am innocent." But even the reporters, normally cool and objective, were caught up in the emotional atmosphere of the scene. Losing the professionalism they should have exhibited, some of them responded angrily with cries of "Coward!" and "Traitor!" and "Dirty Jew!"

Among this group of journalists was Dr. Theodor Herzl, the Paris correspondent for an influential German language newspaper. Herzl, dismayed at these displays of hatred, turned to another reporter and asked about the angry outbursts against Dreyfus. The answer he received stunned him. "They see him not as a human being but as a Jew. Christian compassion ends before it reaches the Jew. It is unjust but we cannot change it. It has always been so and it will be so forever." Those words and the anti-Semitic aspects of the ceremony affected Herzl for the rest of his life. He founded the political Zionist movement which fifty years later, in 1948, led to the re-establishment of the Jewish homeland in Palestine—the modern State of Israel.

As the ceremony ended, the former captain stopped for a brief moment. His eyes focused on the military decorations, ripped from his uniform just moments earlier, which now lay heaped on the ground. That was all that remained of a once-promising career. What lay ahead was the grim reality of a life sentence in a remote and desolate island prison.

By nine-twenty the ceremony had concluded. At the courtyard gate, amidst the continuing screams of "Death to the Jew!" from the mob, the prisoner was turned over to the police for an unceremonious trip in an ordinary police van to the Paris Central Prison. As the van crossed over the Seine River on the Alma Bridge, the prisoner caught a last glimpse through a small barred window of the home he had shared lovingly with his wife and children. He later wrote in his diary, "I was leaving all my happiness behind me. My grief bowed me down."

At the prison he was searched, photographed, fingerprinted, and placed in a cell until arrangements were completed to transport him to his final destination, the infamous French prison colony on Devil's Island, thirty miles off the coast of French Guiana in South America.

There was little doubt of the captain's guilt. After all, he had been found guilty of treason against France by the unanimous verdict of a prestigious military court. The faith of France in its army was legendary: although the court proceedings against the captain were conducted in secret, there was no reason to question that the accused had shamelessly betrayed his own country.

Dreyfus was nearly alone in asserting his innocence. Writing to his wife on the day of the degradation ceremony, he could still not believe what had happened to him. "I seemed to be the victim of an hallucination. . . . There is a traitor, but it is not I." In all of France only a handful of people, led primarily by his wife and brother, publicly affirmed faith in Dreyfus's innocence.

There were, however, some unanswered questions. If, for example, the captain was really guilty, why did he protest so much? As the reporter for *The New York Times* pointed out in his coverage of the ceremony, "Generally, ninety-nine of every hundred men who are thus degraded weep like children, but Dreyfus was firm throughout. He appeared to be less affected than almost any other person present."

Then, there was the Jewish question. Why was so much attention paid to the captain's religion? From the beginning, it was not the guilt or innocence of one army officer that mattered.

19

After the degradation ceremony in 1895, Dreyfus is shown entering a coach on his way to the Paris Central Prison.

For it was not Dreyfus the French army captain who was on trial, but Dreyfus the Jew. And to a large proportion of the general public (and an even larger proportion of French army officers), Dreyfus's Jewishness was enough to make him guilty without any question.

As Captain Alfred Dreyfus languished in a vermin-infested cell far away on Devil's Island, the question of his guilt or innocence began to absorb all of France. In the years that followed, France would find itself consumed with the case of the Jewish army captain. It was now not a simple matter of treason but a complicated saga of blind passion, subverted justice, and shameless bigotry. The rest of the world watched in disbelief as France, the country that gave democracy to Europe, became totally absorbed by The Dreyfus Affair.

From 1894 through 1906, and for years beyond, two factors would blow this event totally out of proportion and engage an entire country in bitter and divisive debate. First, Captain Dreyfus happened to be Jewish, the only Jew on the army General Staff. Second, and most important, he was innocent of all the charges brought against him.

· TWO ·

The Bordereau

As to the traitor, there he is. I swear it!
—*Major Henry*

IT WAS no accident that the German Embassy had the cleanest wastebaskets in all Paris. To the embassy staff Madame Marie Bastian was a most efficient and loyal worker—the best cleaning lady ever. Little did her satisfied employers know that to the officers of the French Intelligence Service she was known by the code name "Auguste"—the best spy ever.

Agent "Auguste" cleaned the embassy in a most thorough manner; she gave special attention to the office and living quarters of the German military attaché, Colonel Maximilian von Schwarzkoppen. She carefully scooped up torn and burned papers from the fireplaces and wastebaskets. Then, on a regular schedule she visited Sainte Clothilde or one of the other local churches and delivered them to an equally "devout" French Intelligence officer.

After each delivery of torn scraps, officers of the "Statistical Section," the army General Staff's Intelligence Service, would spend days and sometimes weeks painstakingly fitting the tiny pieces of paper together. But the effort was worthwhile. In the several years that Madame Bastian was on the job, the French learned important German secrets.

In one such intercepted message, they discovered that a Frenchman, referred to only as "the scoundrel D—," had provided the Germans with military information. They could not find out who he was.

Sometime during September of 1894 another packet of informative scraps arrived through Madame Bastian. Major Hubert Henry, an officer in the Statistical Section, dumped all the bits and pieces of paper onto a large table and began the slow task of fitting them together. One item soon stood out among the rest. It was a bordereau, or covering letter, written on a very thin special paper used in foreign correspondence, much like modern onion skin or airmail paper. Handwritten on the sheet was a list of five top secret French military documents the writer had already provided Colonel Schwarzkoppen.

I have no news that you wish to see me; however, I am sending you some interesting information:

1. A note on the hydraulic brake of the 120 mm. gun and the way in which it worked.
2. A note on the supporting troops. Some modifications will be made by a new plan.
3. A note on the modification of artillery formations.
4. A note concerning Madagascar.
5. The projected Firing Manual for Field Artillery (March 14, 1894).

There was no trace of the documents themselves. By now, they were probably in Berlin. The writer ended by noting, "I'm about to go off to maneuvers."

Major Henry was alarmed. After sharing the information with other officers of the Statistical Section, he took the list to Commandant Jean Sandherr, the head of the Intelligence Service.

Sandherr lost no time. He had photographs of the bordereau distributed to all offices of the General Staff. Perhaps someone could recognize the handwriting. No one did.

On October 6, Lieutenant Colonel the Marquis Albert d'Aboville returned from vacation to a new position as deputy chief of the General Staff's Fourth Bureau. The head of the bureau, Colonel Fabre, informed d'Aboville about the puzzling case and showed him a photograph of the bordereau. To the new man the solution was quite simple. With a confident look he told his chief that the culprit was certainly one of the General Staff trainees.

Each new officer on the General Staff went through a series of "stages" or assignments which gave him experience in each of the four bureaus. Since the information on the bordereau came from several of the bureaus, the spy, "the scoundrel D—," had to be one of the trainees. Colonel Fabre nodded. Of course, there was the answer. So simple. Reading down a list of current trainees, one name stood out—Captain Alfred Dreyfus. He was the only Jewish officer on the General Staff and his name began with "D." Taking a sample of the captain's handwriting from the files, the two officers came to the conclusion that it was similar to the writing on the bordereau.

D'Aboville was pleased with himself. Only his first day on the new job and he had already proven himself to his superior. Never mind that the bordereau made mention of the writer going off to maneuvers and that none of the trainees had gone that year!

News of the finding made its way up the chain of command. Sandherr, the Intelligence chief, breathed a sigh of relief. "I should have known it!" he agreed. The minister of war, General Auguste Mercier, was shaken. This news in the hands of political enemies could be disastrous to his career. Now, however, he would get credit for routing an important traitor. But first, the case had to be perfectly airtight. If they accused the wrong man, it would be political suicide for the minister.

The information given to the Germans was so secret it could only have come from within the army's General Staff. The traitor must be caught! Quickly, he gave orders to Sandherr and his staff to "get to the bottom of the case immediately."

An officer of the Third Bureau, Major Mercier du Paty de Clam, a relative of General Raoul de Boisdeffre, head of the General Staff, was selected to conduct the investigation. Partially chosen because his hobby was graphology—the study of handwriting—du Paty compared the handwritings. Although there were "certain differences," he reported that Dreyfus's handwriting belonged "to the same family" as the writing on the bordereau. To the General Staff officers, that was good enough. Dreyfus was certainly the traitor!

A confession by Dreyfus at this point would firm up the case. Mercier ordered du Paty to arrest the traitor. Du Paty relished the role of amateur detective and developed the "perfect" plan to extract a confession.

For the Dreyfus family, the weekend of October 13 and 14, 1894, was routinely quiet. A time for relaxation and informality for Alfred, his wife, Lucie, and their children, Pierre and Jeanne. The only out-of-the-ordinary event was an early Saturday message summoning Alfred to an inspection the following Monday morning. The timing of this routine notice was puzzling since no one usually worked at the General Staff during the weekend. More surprising to Dreyfus was the order for him to appear in civilian dress. But, orders were orders, and the weekend relaxation with family continued. On Sunday evening, Dreyfus and his wife dined leisurely at the home of his in-laws.

On Monday morning, October 15, 1894, dressed in a simple brown suit, Captain Dreyfus kissed his three-year-old son,

Pierre, and stepped out onto the Avenue du Trocadéro. It was a cold, bright day and Dreyfus walked briskly across the Alma Bridge—his daily route to work. Today, however, would prove to be far from routine.

Arriving a bit early at headquarters, the captain chatted pleasantly with a former instructor of his, Major Georges Picquart. At nine, the two men strolled casually toward the office of the chief of staff, General Raoul de Boisdeffre, and then separated. Dreyfus found four men waiting for him in the general's office. Major du Paty de Clam, the only man in uniform, received him. The others, unidentified, stood in the background. Their identities would soon become clear. They were Inspector Armand Cochefort of the police, his assistant, and Felix Gribelin, archivist of the Statistical Section. Hidden out of sight, carefully watching every move, was Major Hubert Henry.

"The general is on his way," du Paty explained. Then he made a strange request of the captain. "My finger is sore and I have to write a letter for the general. Will you write it for me?" Dreyfus, puzzled, sat down at a little table. Du Paty took a seat directly opposite and riveted his eyes on Dreyfus's hand. The dictation began. Later, Dreyfus learned that the dictated words were carefully chosen from the bordereau so they could be matched to the handwriting. Du Paty watched every movement and gesture Dreyfus made for some telltale sign that the suspect recognized the words and thereby proved his guilt.

Midway during the dictation, Major du Paty suddenly shouted at Dreyfus in an accusatory manner, "You are trembling, Captain!"

"No," responded the startled writer, who offered a simple explanation. "My fingers are cold."

"Pay attention, Captain, this is serious," scolded the major and continued to the end of the strange dictation.

With the writing concluded, du Paty jumped from his seat and placed his hand on the captain's shoulder. Speaking in a loud voice he dramatically proclaimed: "In the name of the law, I arrest you! You are accused of the crime of high treason." Shaken, Dreyfus stumbled from his seat, protesting his innocence. What was happening to him?

Inspector Cochefort and his assistant stepped forward, grabbed Dreyfus, and searched his pockets. "Take my keys, open everything in my house: I am innocent," Dreyfus protested. "You won't find anything, only I beg you, exercise discretion with my wife."

As the initial shock wore off, Dreyfus began to think rationally. "At least show me the evidence," he demanded.

Without giving any details of the exact charges, du Paty curtly answered, "The evidence is overwhelming." Demanding an immediate confession, du Paty theatrically placed a loaded pistol on the table. The message was clear. An "honorable" traitor, once discovered, should either confess or kill himself. To du Paty's dismay, Dreyfus steadfastly did neither. But that did not matter. After all, there was no doubt of this man's guilt.

Major Henry emerged from the shadows and escorted a still disbelieving Dreyfus to the Cherche-Midi military prison. There, Lieutenant Colonel d'Aboville had made secret arrangements with the director, Major Ferdinand Forzinetti, to receive a special prisoner, a Jewish General Staff officer guilty of treason. Because of the delicate nature of the crime, no news of the officer's arrest was to be released, not even to Forzinetti's superiors. Furthermore, the prisoner was to be placed in an isolated cell and have no contact with the outside world. "The Jews will leave no stone unturned to find out where Dreyfus is," d'Aboville pointedly warned the prison director.

By now, Dreyfus, normally calm and unexcitable, was an emotional wreck. Alone in his cell, he acted like a madman, overturning furniture, pounding his head against the stone cell wall and sobbing uncontrollably. Forzinetti was alarmed and entered the cell to offer support. He spoke gently to his prisoner and reasoned with him. In time, Dreyfus quieted down. To Forzinetti, a hardened observer of criminal behavior, the distressed man in front of him could not be guilty of such a horrible crime.

Meanwhile, counting on the element of surprise, du Paty went to search the Dreyfus home. There he hoped to find the same unusual paper on which the bordereau was written or other evidence linking Dreyfus with the Germans. Then, Dreyfus's guilt would be confirmed without a doubt.

The sight of a uniformed officer at her door frightened Lucie. "Is my husband dead?" she asked in alarm.

"No, Madame, worse than that," du Paty replied.

"A fall from a horse?" she nervously suggested.

"No," du Paty continued in a firm voice, "he has been arrested and is in prison on serious charges."

Lucie Dreyfus stood as if thunderstruck as du Paty presented the search warrant. Nothing was found that in any way showed Alfred Dreyfus to be a traitor: no special paper, no contacts with the German Embassy, no financial problems. These facts did not, in the slightest way, disturb du Paty's predetermined belief in the captain's guilt. Turning to the petrified woman, the major ominously declared, "A word, Madame, a single word from you and your husband is irretrievably lost. The sole means of saving him is—silence."

As directed, Lucie with difficulty kept word of the arrest from family and friends. To the children, too young to suspect anything amiss, their father was away on army business.

Alfred was experiencing an agony of a different sort as Major du Paty became an almost daily visitor. The first visit occurred three days after the arrest as Dreyfus lay alone, demoralized and forlorn in his cell. Throwing cut-up photographs of the bordereau and letters written in Dreyfus's own hand on the table, the major ordered Dreyfus to pick out those pieces which contained his own handwriting. Dreyfus accomplished this task with ease, never once picking a piece of the bordereau.

Handwriting of Alfred Dreyfus, as published in a Parisian magazine, comparing his handwriting with that on the bordereau.

During other visits, du Paty dictated sentences and phrases from the bordereau and forced Dreyfus to write them down in odd positions while sitting, lying down, or standing. He was hoping in some way to trap the captain into duplicating the handwriting on the bordereau. Again and again du Paty questioned Dreyfus.

The tormented captain was near insanity not hearing from his family or even being told the specific charges against him. Pushing back thoughts of suicide he lectured himself. "If you die, they will believe you guilty: whatever happens, you must live to cry aloud your innocence in the face of the world." In spite of the brave thoughts, Dreyfus was near the breaking point. At times he would cry, yell, and laugh hysterically. His only comfort came from Forzinetti, who was so alarmed at Dreyfus's worsening physical and mental health that on October 24 he requested permission from the minister of war to send a doctor to treat the prisoner. Not until October 29, two weeks after the arrest, did du Paty finally show Dreyfus a photograph of the bordereau. Ironically, the sight of that document made Dreyfus feel better: what court could possibly find him guilty on such flimsy evidence?

Unknown to the prisoner, the minister of war shared the same thoughts about the bordereau. Before proceeding with further action, he needed to be completely sure that the handwriting on the bordereau was Dreyfus's. On October 12 he turned to a real handwriting expert, Alfred Gobert of the Bank of France. Gobert's response was even weaker than that of the hobbyist du Paty. After carefully examining the two documents he simply reported that the bordereau could have been written by someone else. This less-than-definitive report did not please Mercier.

Another opinion was necessary; one which more directly confirmed the guilt of the Jewish officer. Alphonse Bertillon, although a noted criminologist, had little experience in evaluating handwriting. Yet he did not hesitate to provide the desired opinion. "If we set aside the idea of a document forged with the greatest care, it is manifestly evident that the same person has written all the papers given for examination, including the incriminating document." No one could make any sense out of the reasoning that led to his conclusion, but that did not matter. After all, he did say that both documents were written by the same person.

But the word of one expert might not be enough. Mercier asked the prefect of police to find three other experts to analyze the bordereau. Their results were inconclusive. One quickly announced that the handwritings were not the same. The other two, who had consulted with Bertillon, reached different conclusions. The first declared that the handwriting was the same; the other hedged his report by saying that it was "probable" that the handwritings were the same.

Although rumors had begun to surface, the arrest was still kept secret so that sufficient evidence against Dreyfus could be collected. Too much was at stake. Major du Paty had no doubts about the guilt of the prisoner. Yet even he recognized the weakness of a case based solely on the bordereau. Like Mercier, he *knew* instinctively that Dreyfus was guilty; only the proof was lacking. Secrecy was needed to avoid political embarrassment should the army decide not to prosecute. On October 31 a discouraged du Paty asked Mercier if the case should be dropped. But, it was now too late. A new element was now involved—the press.

La Libre Parole, the anti-Semitic newspaper edited by Edouard Drumont, had in recent weeks been waging a war of words words against Mercier. The focus of this attack was the presence of Jewish officers in the army: to the anti-Semites they were an affront to the French nation and should be removed. That complaint was only an indication of the widespread anti-Jewish feeling common in France at the time. This deeply rooted hatred and distrust of Jews was firmly ingrained in the hearts and minds of many Frenchmen. So they did not find it difficult to look upon their Jewish neighbors as "outsiders" capable of committing all sorts of treasonable acts against their country.

On October 28, a letter arrived at the newspaper with the information that ". . . it is Captain Dreyfus who lives at 6 Avenue du Trocadéro, who was arrested on the fifteenth as a spy and who is now in the Cherche-Midi prison. . . . All Israel is up in arms." Where did the information come from? The note was simply signed, "Henry."

The next day a short question appeared in the newspaper asking if it were true that the army was involved in an important arrest. Other newspapers quickly caught scent of the developing story, and it became the talk of the country. When Drumont ran a special banner headline in the November 1 edition of *La Libre Parole,* it was received as certain truth in many circles. "HIGH TREASON," the headline roared, "ARREST OF A JEWISH OFFICER, CAPTAIN DREYFUS."

Once the prisoner's name was publicly known, Major du Paty finally permitted Lucie to contact her husband's family in Mulhouse. The captain was still kept in solitary confinement. Immediately upon receipt of the telegram from Lucie, Alfred's brother Mathieu was on his way to Paris. He found a city overcome with rabid hatred of his brother, and Jews in general, fueled by the increasingly shrill newspapers of all political persuasions. Every whispered rumor soon appeared in print as a fact of absolute truth. No story about the traitor was too far-fetched to print. In a matter-of-fact way, the Catholic newspaper, *La Croix,* reported, "Dreyfus is an agent of international Jewry."

Finding a lawyer to represent Alfred Dreyfus was not easy. Some were afraid of damage to their political careers if their names were associated with a publicly accused Jewish traitor. Mathieu finally persuaded a respected Catholic attorney, Edgar Demange, to take the case. Demange agreed to this only after carefully reading the records and speaking to the accused. Like

Captain Dreyfus, he did not see how anyone could be convicted on such flimsy evidence.

The public prosecutor, on the other hand, had a different opinion of the evidence: to him, the testimony of the handwriting experts was crucial. Major Bexon d'Ormescheville zealously undertook his official examinations to prepare for the court-martial.

Only with the trial date finally set was Dreyfus allowed to communicate with his wife—by mail. Each tried to cheer up the other. Dreyfus had the utmost confidence in military justice. "Tomorrow I shall appear before my judges, my head held high, my soul tranquil. I am ready to appear before soldiers as a soldier who has nothing with which to reproach himself. They will see in my face, they will read in my soul, they will know that I am innocent, as all will know who know me."

The trial opened on December 19, 1894, at the Cherche-Midi prison. Despite strong objections from Demange, the court ruled the trial would be conducted in secret. Aside from the seven army officers who acted as judges, the only others in the room were Dreyfus, Demange, the prosecuting attorney, and two men whose presence was quite unusual. The first was the prefect of police; the other, Major Georges Picquart, the officer who walked Dreyfus to his appointment that fateful Monday morning. Picquart was there under orders to report on the trial directly to the minister of war and the army chief of staff. Little did Picquart then realize the significant role he would later play in Dreyfus's life. Witnesses would be called as needed.

General Mercier, the minister of war, was concerned about the trial. He understood that in an ordinary court of law the questionable evidence against Dreyfus would lead to a not guilty verdict. But this was a military court, and although the judges were all honorable men, they had an ingrained bias to protect the honor of the army whose uniforms they so proudly wore.

Before the trial began, the minister had ordered Colonel

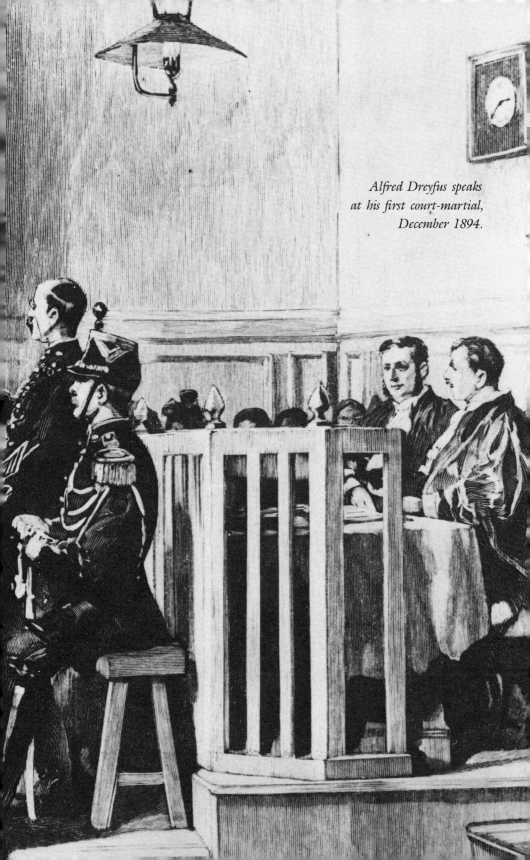

Alfred Dreyfus speaks at his first court-martial, December 1894.

Sandherr and Major du Paty to compile a secret file of documents, statements, and reports which could be used against Dreyfus. In their zeal, the intelligence officers inserted anything remotely related to the Dreyfus case, even going so far as to add forged material to incriminate the defendant.

The court heard the conflicting testimony of the three handwriting experts. Du Paty was called to the stand and told of the dictation incident where he saw the prisoner's hand "tremble." Bertillon, the criminologist, then proceeded to confuse the court with a convoluted theory of how Dreyfus could have forged his own handwriting on the bordereau. Major Henry spoke of the work done by the Statistical Section.

The case against Dreyfus was still not convincing enough. That news was reported to Mercier and Sandherr by Major Picquart. Major Henry made arrangements with one of the judges to be recalled as a witness. In a direct manner he announced that an "honorable person" had alerted his department about a spy on the General Staff. He was referring to a letter sent by a foreign diplomat warning that there was a spy close to the French General Staff. Dreyfus's name was not mentioned in it.

Then, turning dramatically to Dreyfus, Henry pointed his finger at the prisoner and proclaimed, "As to the traitor, there he is!" Dreyfus and Demange both jumped to their feet in objection to demand the name of the informant. The witness responded simply by saying he could not divulge the name. "There are secrets in an officer's head that he does not even tell his cap," Henry explained. The president of the court then asked, "Do you affirm on your honor that the treasonous officer was Captain Dreyfus?" Henry turned deliberately to the crucifix on the wall and raised his right hand. "I swear it!" he responded with firm conviction.

The trial came to an end after four days of testimony on December 22. Aside from Henry's dramatic appearance and the less-than-unanimous testimonies of the handwriting experts, the case against Dreyfus was weak. It was time for Mercier to make use of the secret file. As the court adjourned to allow the judges to deliberate on the verdict, Major du Paty threaded his way through the crowded courtroom. In his hand was a sealed envelope from Colonel Sandherr which he handed to the president of the court-martial. In it was a covering letter signed by the minister of war and several falsified documents from the secret file designed to prove the guilt of Alfred Dreyfus.

Among the misleading documents were: a false biography of Dreyfus which claimed he had been a German spy for years, a letter from Schwarzkoppen referring to "the scoundrel D—," and a deliberate mistranslation by du Paty of a telegram sent to Rome by Panizzardi, the Italian military attaché stating, "Captain Dreyfus is arrested. Precautions taken. Emissary warned." The judges were dramatically influenced by this information.

They had no way of knowing that the documents were either false, irrelevant, or improper. They were loyal army officers with the utmost faith in their superiors. The illegality of withholding secret evidence from the accused did not concern them. After a short deliberation, Captain Alfred Dreyfus was found guilty. His punishment—public degradation and life imprisonment in a remote fortified place. The secret file was immediately handed back to Major du Paty.

Dreyfus could not believe the verdict. He was stunned and shaken. "I am innocent!" he cried helplessly. "I am innocent! My God, you have condemned an innocent man!" Outside, a jubilant mob began a celebration which would last far into the night. "Long live the army! Long live France! Down with the Jews! Death to the traitor!" they shouted over and over.

When Major du Paty returned the secret file to Generals Mercier and de Boisdeffre, Mercier ordered Sandherr and du Paty to remove the items from the file and scatter them to other folders. Sandherr did not obey the order. Perhaps anticipating a future need to protect his own actions, he took the documents and locked them away in a safe.

Dreyfus was wildly agitated by the time he was returned to

Alfred Dreyfus receiving the sentence of the court-martial, 1894.

his cell. In a state of utter defeat, he pleaded for a revolver with which to end his life. Seeing that his cries were in vain, he began ramming his head against the cell wall with such force that Forzinetti was hurriedly summoned before the prisoner could kill himself. As before, the jailer succeeded in calming Dreyfus by imploring him to think of his family and the future. Were he to kill himself now, Forzinetti cautioned, he would only confirm his guilt to the world. "My only crime is to be born a Jew," Dreyfus sobbed.

The distraught captain did not know that the lack of a confession bothered others in the case, too. On December 31, the same day that a routine appeal of Dreyfus's sentence was denied, the prisoner had an unexpected visitor, du Paty de Clam. The officer arrived on orders of superiors to obtain even the slightest hint of a confession from the condemned man. Any such statement would be rewarded by some easing of the sentence. Dreyfus responded only by asking that his case not be forgotten and that the search continue for the real criminal. To that, a shaken du Paty could only mumble, "If you are innocent, you are the greatest martyr of all time."

The French press had covered the arrest and trial with great detail and relish. Readers enjoyed a good scandal! Some newspapers called for Dreyfus's death while others reported on fictitious love affairs. The nature of the crime, treason by a General Staff officer, led to widespread foreign reporting of the case, rumors and all. *The New York Times,* for example, on November 16, 1894, reported that Dreyfus was involved in a spy network with two arrested Germans. The Dreyfus name was famous throughout the world.

· THREE ·

A Bright Future

Everything in life seemed to smile on me.
—*Alfred Dreyfus*

ALFRED DREYFUS was born on October 9, 1859, in Mulhouse, a
city in the northeastern French province of Alsace, not far from
the German border. The close-knit and supportive family of Raphael and Jeanne Dreyfus and their seven children was well-to-
do and respected. Raphael had begun a modest textile business,
which, by the time Alfred was born, had become very successful.
Alfred would always remember his early years with affection.
"My childhood," he said, "passed happily amid the gentle influences of mother and sisters, a kind father devoted to his children,
and the companionship of older brothers."

Alfred, the youngest child, was closest to his oldest sister,
Henriette. She was primarily responsible for raising him, since
their mother was sickly and could not fully attend to the young
child. Alfred, quiet and studious, looked up to his older brother
Mathieu, who was outgoing and athletic. Growing up amid the

40

security and comfort of his loving family, Alfred early displayed a marked sensitivity toward righting wrongs and a concern with being an honorable person. His friends called him "Don Quixote," after the fictional Spanish hero who championed honorable but losing causes. He was a quiet child who spent a lot of time by himself and showed little interest in sports and outdoor games. In short, aside from a shy nature, his life was typical for a boy growing up in an upper-middle-class Jewish family of the time.

For the Jews of France, life had not always been this positive. As in most European countries, Jewish people endured periods of vile discrimination interrupted by interludes of relative tranquility. It was only with the French Revolution of 1789 that a pattern of gradually emerging equality began for the Jews of France. With the granting of full citizenship in 1791, it still took decades more for Jews to receive all the rights other Frenchmen held.

Only in 1831, for example, was Judaism placed on an equal footing with Catholicism and Protestantism and received state financial support for its clergy and houses of worship. By 1850 the Jewish population of France was approximately 75,000. Most Jews, like the Dreyfus family, lived in the Alsace and Lorraine regions. Most were self-employed as merchants or in the professions. They were proud of their French citizenship and were largely assimilated in their local communities. Although deep-rooted anti-Semitism still existed in the country, Jews made noteworthy advances in government service, education, and the military during the decades that followed.

With harsh economic conditions and increased religious persecution in Eastern Europe, thousands of other Jews began moving into Western Europe. In France, many flooded into the crowded older sections of Paris. Their quaint dress and strict adherence to Jewish law set them apart from other residents as well as from the long-assimilated and established French-Jewish community. To the growing number of anti-Semites these newcomers conveniently and pointedly represented all Jews as outsiders and natural enemies, responsible for all that was wrong with French society. Everywhere they looked, the anti-Semites seemed to find "evidence" of Jewish plots and syndicates against French people and culture.

By the 1860s France and other European countries began looking nervously at the growing strength of their German neighbor. There, formerly independent states were being unified under the leadership of Otto von Bismarck of Prussia. "The great questions of the day," he said, "are not decided by speeches and majority votes, but by blood and iron." By 1867, Bismarck succeeded in uniting the northern German states into a powerful North German Confederation. He now only needed to convince the southern states to join and his dream of a united Germany would come true.

A threat of war from a neighboring country seemed a good way to coax the remaining German states into a union. France seemed the perfect target. Napoleon III, nephew of the first Napoleon, had been emperor of France since 1852. He was a flamboyant if not erratic leader, but he had turned France into an economic and international power rivaled only by the new German confederation. In a series of brilliant diplomatic moves, Bismarck succeeded in backing Napoleon III into a situation where France had no choice but to declare war on Germany or lose respect as a nation at home and abroad. French public opinion reached fever pitch as Napoleon declared war on Prussia on July 19, 1870.

The Franco-Prussian War was a disaster for France. Poorly equipped and led, the French army was quickly battered on all fronts by the disciplined and efficient Prussian troops. For Alfred Dreyfus, then just eleven years old, talk of war was exciting while the sight of smartly uniformed French soldiers marching off to war made his heart pound with patriotism. Pride soon turned to despair, however, as the same troops returned in torn and bloody uniforms, utterly defeated and humiliated.

On September 2, Napoleon III, who was personally leading the troops, surrendered himself and his army to the victorious Otto von Bismarck. When news of this tragic defeat reached Paris, a new government was proclaimed to continue the war. This marked the beginning of France's Third Republic, which would last through World War II. The Germans soon reached the outskirts of Paris and laid siege to the city from September 23 to January 28. An armistice agreement was finally reached and the fighting ended. To France's ultimate humiliation, the Treaty of Frankfurt (May 10, 1871), which marked the official end of the war, annexed the French Alsace and Lorraine regions to Germany and required France to pay Germany a five-billion-franc indemnity or compensation.

The annexation permitted the residents of the region to either remain in their homes as German citizens or retain their French citizenship but leave Alsace. The Dreyfus family, like other Alsatian families, had a momentous decision to make. For Raphael Dreyfus there really was no choice. He was a loyal Frenchman. Choosing to retain French citizenship for himself and his family, he left Mulhouse in October 1872 for nearby Basel, Switzerland. Only his eldest son, Jacques, remained behind as a German citizen to watch over the family's factories and business interests. A few years later the family received special permission from the Germans to return to Mulhouse as French citizens. Jacques, in 1897, returned to French citizenship, too, by opening a branch of the business in France.

This was a trying time for young Alfred. First, his beloved sister, Henriette, with whom he had been so close, had married and moved away from Mulhouse in 1870. Now, as the result of war, he found himself living in a Swiss city where German and not French was heard on the streets. The patriotic boy seethed with anger over the humiliation and embarrassment all France suffered. He would later say, "The painful recollection has never faded from my memory."

In Basel, Alfred attended the Realschule, where he experienced problems. Besides the normal adjustment to a new way of life, the language of instruction was German, with which he had great difficulty. For the next school year his parents decided to send Alfred to a boarding school, Collège Sainte Barbe, in Paris. The idea of placing him in a French school might have been a good one but did not take the boy's personal needs into consideration. Alfred could not adapt to life in this strictly run school and made no friends. When he became sick midyear, his family brought him home.

Alfred was sent back to Paris for the 1874 school year. Only this time it was to a different, more liberal school, Collège Chaptal, where he gained a reputation as a serious student but also as somewhat of a bore. Nonetheless he graduated successfully in 1876 and returned to the Collège Sainte Barbe for an additional year of study to prepare for the entrance examination to the École Polytechnique, the French military engineering school. Admission was highly selective yet he applied himself with intensity and was successful. He ranked 182 in an entering class of 236 students.

Young Alfred had dreamed of entering the army since childhood. Now he could prepare for the time when a rebuilt, reorganized French army could redeem its honor and obtain revenge from the Germans. His family was not entirely keen upon Alfred entering the army. Yet they did not stand in his way and were even proud of the fact that their son, a Jew, was demonstrating the loyalty to France they all felt. Upon his graduation in 1880, the young French army second lieutenant was sent to Fontainebleau for further training at the School of Instruction. His dream had come true.

After graduation, Alfred was promoted to first lieutenant and posted to the Thirty-first Artillery Regiment at LeMans. He had a successful first year as an officer and was rewarded with a choice assignment in Paris with the First Cavalry Division. He was then only twenty-four years old. During the next five years he gained a reputation as a good horseman and leader. But he never really fit in with the other junior officers, who considered him stuffy and aloof. While his colleagues spent their free time drinking and gambling, the serious-minded Dreyfus read, studied, and kept to himself.

Alfred enjoyed spending his furlough times at home with his family. Yet it angered him that he needed permission from the German government to visit his beloved Mulhouse, now known by the German name of Mülhausen. On one of these home visits, the French officer in civilian dress watched sadly as a celebration took place marking the anniversary of Napoleon III's defeat in the Franco-Prussian War.

In 1889, at age thirty, his diligence was recognized with another promotion. With the rank of captain Alfred Dreyfus was sent to the École Centrale de Pyrotechnie Militaire in Bourges. He immersed himself in more study. His goal now was to gain admission to the École de Guerre, France's prestigious War College. Acceptance was highly selective, especially for Jewish officers. But successful graduates were assured of promising futures at the top leadership level of the French army.

Looking for ways to increase his chances of acceptance to the École de Guerre, Alfred sought out the Hadamard family of Paris on the suggestion of one of Mathieu's friends. The Hadamards, of Alsatian background like Dreyfus, were one of France's leading Jewish families. Mr. Hadamard was a well-known Paris jeweler whose father had been a noted army officer and graduate of the École de Guerre. Both he and his wife welcomed Captain Dreyfus to their home and offered useful advice to the aspiring officer. There, Alfred met and quickly fell in love with their young and attractive daughter, Lucie. Shortly after Alfred and Lucie first met, Alfred's long-ailing mother died.

The young couple had much in common. They shared the same backgrounds. Both seemed outwardly shy and withdrawn but in private were really sophisticated and witty. The wedding took place on April 21, 1890. Just one day earlier, Alfred received the joyful news that he had been admitted to the École de Guerre.

Alfred and Lucie rented a spacious apartment at 6 Avenue du Trocadéro, not far from the War College, which was located in the shadow of the Eiffel Tower at the École Militaire. For the next two years Alfred devoted himself totally to his studies. He felt driven to do better than his classmates, since he did not have their social and family connections to rely on. He could concentrate exclusively on school because he had no outside worries. Financially, he and Lucie were well off, due in part to the yearly royalty he earned from part ownership of the family business. Their apartment was nicely furnished and there was always domestic help.

The Dreyfuses entertained little and had few close friends. Their daily schedule was military-like in its unvarying routine. On Sundays, they regularly dined at the Hadamards. The routine changed somewhat on April 5, 1891, when their son, Pierre, was born. The child brought the Dreyfus household to life and their social life picked up. They became part of a small social circle which included the Chief Rabbi of France, Zadok Cohen, and his wife.

At school, Alfred worked harder than ever to remain right at the top of his class. Life revolved around the War College and his home. It wasn't just pride that motivated him but the knowledge that the top graduates of every class were invited to serve as probationary officers on the army General Staff.

No matter how hard Alfred tried to isolate himself from the outside world, he could not long ignore the anti-Semitism that was rampant in French society. Foremost among the leading anti-Semites was Edouard-Adolphe Drumont. His book, *La France Juive* (Jewish France), which first appeared in 1886, quickly became one of the most popular books of the entire nineteenth century. The Jews, Drumont wrote, were responsible for all the ills that affected France. Whatever political, economic, or behavioral complaints people could think of, Drumont blamed on the Jews. His growing number of readers believed, without any doubt, that Jews were not only evil but were continually plotting to undermine the lives of all "decent" Frenchmen.

An example was the Panama Canal Scandal. A company had been formed in France to build a canal through the isthmus of Panama, shortening the trip from the Atlantic to the Pacific oceans. The idea was sensational and popular. Thousands of hardworking French people invested their life savings in this "can't fail" company with the hope of making huge profits. When the Panama Canal Company suddenly went bankrupt in 1889, all of France was thrown into turmoil.

Although later investigation would show that the entire company was corrupt, there were several Jews on the board of directors. Drumont and other anti-Semites raised shrill cries against "wicked Jewish financiers" who took advantage of honest, unsuspecting, and decent French citizens. This, of course, was a lie. But to the French, who were conditioned to anti-Semitism, it was undebatable truth.

The hatred continued in the columns of Drumont's *La Libre Parole,* whose fiery articles complained about the Jewish presence in the army. The paper published the names of Jewish officers and accused them of treason. The result was a series of duels involving Jewish officers. In one duel, Edouard Drumont was challenged by a Jewish officer, Captain Cremieux-Foa. One of the Jewish officer's seconds was Major Walsin Esterhazy, soon to occupy an important place in the life of Alfred Dreyfus. Another duel ended tragically with the death of a Jewish officer, Captain Armand Meyer. The resulting public indignation and the strong protests by the French government were enough to force Drumont to tone down his attacks.

But not even Dreyfus could escape the residual bigotry. By his calculations, Alfred ranked third in his class, a position high enough that he could not be denied a probationer's place on the General Staff. When the final grades were posted, Dreyfus and another Jewish officer found themselves ranked lower than expected due to adverse reports by General Bonnefond, who believed that "Jews were not desired" on the General Staff. Both Jewish candidates appealed to General Lebelin de Dionne, who, while expressing regret, said he could not change the original report. In November 1892, Alfred Dreyfus graduated ninth out of a class of eighty-one, which still allowed his appointment as a probationer with the General Staff effective January 1, 1893.

With the new year came other changes, as well. His beloved father, from whom he had inherited his strong French patriotism, died in January. In February, Alfred and Lucie's second child, a daughter whom they named Jeanne, was born.

In 1893 and 1894 Captain Alfred Dreyfus went through the "stages" of a probational officer on the French Army General Staff. The General Staff was divided into four separate bureaus, each with a different responsibility. The First Bureau dealt with organization and mobilization of troops, the Second Bureau with intelligence operations. The Third Bureau dealt with military operations and training, and the Fourth Bureau with communications and transport. By giving each probationer experience in all four bureaus, a candidate received an in-depth tour of important General Staff departments.

Service in each of these "stages" also gave superior officers a chance to observe the probationers and rate them for ultimate career assignments. These young officers were, after all, the brightest and ablest in the entire French army. Dreyfus received high ratings at each stage with the exception of the Fourth Bureau, whose head, Colonel Fabre, was an outspoken anti-Semite. The probationers did not go through the stages in any order, so in July 1894, Dreyfus was assigned to the Third Bureau.

Dreyfus later described this period in his life optimistically. "A brilliant and easy career was open to me: my future seemed most auspicious. After work I found rest and delight at home. I had no material cares. . . . Everything in life seemed to smile on me."

· FOUR ·

Cut Off from the World

My only crime is to have been born a Jew. —*Alfred Dreyfus*

WITH THE end of the trial, Dreyfus received a shattering preview of the rest of his life. Taken to the Santé prison to await deportation, he was no longer treated civilly as an accused officer but harshly as a convicted traitor. At least he was permitted to see Lucie again, twice a week, but only under the strictest supervision. On January 2, when they saw each other for the first time since October, they were not allowed to kiss or even touch. Their brief meetings were monitored by a prison official.

Even their heart-wrenching letters were carefully read by the authorities before being passed on. On January 11, Alfred wrote to Lucie. "Upheld by your love, by the devotion of our entire family, I shall overcome fate. I do not say that I shall not have moments of despondency . . . but I shall live, my adored one. . . ." After one of their brief visits, Lucie described her feelings. "The sight of you has done me good: I could not cease looking at and listening to you; but it is horrible to have to leave you alone in your bare cell, a prey to such fearful mental torture, undeserved. . . ."

During the night of January 17, Dreyfus was taken from the jail without warning. He was hustled to a waiting prison train and brutally handcuffed and shackled in an open cell scarcely big enough to hold a seated person. The long journey to the coastal railroad station at La Rochelle was cold and painful. Even when the train pulled into the station at noon the next day, the agony did not end. While Dreyfus languished feverish and hungry in his cramped cell, local people at the station began to notice unusual activity as guards and officials scurried about. An important prisoner must be on that train.

Someone whispered the name Dreyfus, and whatever secrecy the authorities had wanted to maintain was gone. Soon, a sizable crowd gathered as the guards kept Dreyfus confined in his miserable cell. To further torment him, cries of "Death to the Jew!" and "Kill the traitor!" echoed through his bars. By nightfall, when it was clear that the local citizens were not going away, the guards finally escorted the prisoner from the train.

The moment people in the crowd caught sight of the traitor, they rushed forward to curse and throw punches at him. The violence continued until the military escort finally threw Dreyfus into a carriage which took him to the docks. Then, it was another hour by launch to the Île de Ré and the island military prison that was the stopover for convicts sentenced to deportation.

Dreyfus was placed in a cell with a large window-like opening from which guards observed his every movement night and day. Whenever he returned from the allowed daily walk, he was stripped and searched. Lucie, who now had to make the long journey from Paris, was authorized two short visits a week during which she sat at one end of a room and Alfred at the other.

DEPOT DE SAINT-MARTIN-DE-RÉ

le 25 Janvier 1895

Noms et prénoms *Alfred Dreyfus*   Mardi

No d'écrou   Atelier   9ʰ matin

Comme tu dois souffrir !... Le drame dont nous sommes les victimes est certainement le plus épouvantable du siècle. Avoir tout pour toi; bonheur, avenir, intérieur charmant, et puis tout à coup, te voir accusé et condamné pour un crime monstrueux! Ah le monstre qui a jeté ainsi le déshonneur dans une famille aurait mieux fait de me tuer, au moins il n'y aurait que moi qui aurait souffert

Letter written by Dreyfus after his degradation. Written at the prison at the Île de Ré.

In the middle sat the prison director, who carefully observed and heard everything.

The prisoner was limited to writing two letters a week to his wife. Even so, the mail was censored and often withheld. "I have but two happy moments in my days," Alfred wrote. "The first is when they bring me this sheet of paper that I may write you, and I pass a little time in talking to you. The second is when they bring me your daily letter. . . ."

Neither Lucie nor Alfred knew that their February 21 visit would be their last. Immediately after the meeting, Alfred was again brutally stripped and searched and ordered to quickly get his things together. Before he realized what was happening, he found himself on board a transport ship. He still did not know where he was going.

The shivering prisoner huddled on the floor of a cramped cell on the deck of the *Saint-Nazaire*. As frigid blasts of wind ripped through the open grating of the cell door, Alfred Dreyfus could only sob and moan in despair. His ice-cold perception of reality was that he would never see France or his family again.

Guards were stationed twenty-four hours a day at his cell door. They had specific orders never to talk to the prisoner. But from snatches of conversation among the guards, and the fact that the temperature was getting warmer as they approached the equator, Dreyfus knew they were heading toward French Guiana and the coast of South America.

The Îles du Salut (Salvation Islands) are located about twenty-five miles off the coast of French Guiana, just north of the equator. As a penal colony, it provided the government with the ultimate in security, and the unfortunate convicts with the most miserable climate and terrain under French rule.

Dreyfus, regarded as "an embittered criminal, not worthy of any pity," was destined for the smallest of the island chain, Devil's Island, formerly a lepers' colony. Conditions on the island were so unhealthy that the lepers had been removed. The climate was continually humid, with temperatures in July and August hovering above 90 degrees. The rainy seasons were from April through June and then from November through January. Insects and vermin abounded and malaria was a common malady. The island was surrounded by treacherous currents and ferocious sharks. Escape was nearly impossible.

On March 12, 1895, after a grueling fifteen-day crossing, the *Saint-Nazaire* anchored in the harbor. The prisoner was confined to his stifling cell for four days on board ship while the authorities awaited instructions. The work on Dreyfus's living quarters had not yet been completed and the local officials did not know what to do with him. Finally, new orders were received and Dreyfus was taken off the ship and placed in a prison cell on the largest of the islands, the Île Royale. He remained there, locked continually in a shuttered cell, unable to speak with anyone, for one month before he was finally transported to Devil's Island.

His new home was a single-room square hut with an iron-barred door which opened onto a smaller guard booth. The booth, in turn, was closed to the outside by a solid wood door. The prisoner was watched continually. Guards, with strict orders not to address him, were changed every two hours, day and night, to the irritating sounds of clanging keys and scraping feet. The inside of the hut was illuminated all night. Only during the day was Dreyfus allowed to leave the confines of his hut to exercise in a small rectangular space under the watchful eye of an armed guard.

If the purpose of his deportation was punishment, its goal was also to break his spirit. He was treated with the utmost contempt and harshness by his jailers, although he was allowed writing materials and books at first. On April 14, 1895, he began keeping a diary. "I am still in the closest confinement. All my correspondence is read and checked off at the Ministry, and often not forwarded. They even forbid my writing to my wife about the investigations which I wished to counsel her to have made. It is impossible for me to defend myself."

His only means of communication with the outside world was by mail and even that slim thread was manipulated by the authorities. Although letters from Lucie had arrived in Cayenne, the capital of French Guiana, in March, they were returned to France to be censored. Dreyfus did not receive his first letters from his wife until June 12. "The gloomy, monotonous days are hardly distinguishable one from another," he wrote in his diary.

He gradually developed a daily routine. "I rise at daybreak (half-past five) and light my fire and make coffee or tea. Then I put the dried vegetables on the fire, and afterward make my bed, clean my chamber. . . . At eight o'clock they bring me the day's rations. I finish cooking the dried vegetables, and on meat days place these rations on the fire. Thus all my cooking is over by ten o'clock, for I eat in the evening what is left over from the morning. At ten o'clock I lunch. Next I read, work, dream, and most of all, suffer until three o'clock. . . . As soon as the heat has diminished, toward five o'clock, I cut my wood, draw water from the well, wash my linen, and so on. At six o'clock I eat the cold remains of my luncheon. Then I am locked up."

At first, he had no plates, so he used the leftover tin cans which he could never properly clean. As well, he had to wash his own clothes—without being allowed any soap. Only later did the island commandant, showing a little humanity, give him some real plates and occasional treats such as canned milk. Fever was an almost constant companion and, because he hardly ever had the opportunity to talk, he nearly lost his power of speech. "I must pull together all my courage to live under such conditions, added to all my mental tortures. Utterly exhausted, I will stretch out on my bed."

To keep mentally alert, Dreyfus continued to write in his diary and send letters to Lucie. He lived for the infrequent mail he was permitted to receive. Each letter was read carefully for any sign that the true culprit had been found. He read from the books and magazines permitted him and worked at perfecting his English. He exercised whenever he was physically able. When other convicts came to work on the island, Dreyfus was shut up in his hut no matter what the temperature to prevent human contact.

His diary and letters indicate the ups and downs of his mental state. On June 19, he wrote: "I feel myself falling into black depths of despair. Then, I ask myself, what of my poor Lucie and my children? No, I will not abandon them. With all the strength that in me lies, so long as I have a shadow of vitality I will keep faith with those who belong to me. I must make whole my honor and the honor of my children."

Incredibly, his love and devotion to France never wavered. On Bastille Day, July 14, 1895, he wrote in his diary: "I have looked at the tricolor flag floating everywhere, the flag I have loyally served. My pen falls from my fingers. Some feelings cannot be expressed in words."

As time passed, Dreyfus's mental and physical condition deteriorated. He wrote in his diary on May 5, 1896, "I have nothing more to say. All is alike in hideousness! What a horrible life! . . ."

Dreyfus languished on the inhospitable island unaware of what, if anything, was happening in France on his behalf. The delayed and censored mail which reached him could not contain any references at all to his case. He only hoped the outside world would not forget him.

But hope alone cannot guarantee freedom. Since the end of the trial both Lucie and his older brother Mathieu had been using every means at their disposal to keep interest alive in a case the army was content to forget. Mathieu Dreyfus spoke to any politician or journalist who would listen. At first he did not know any details about his brother's alleged crime and had no proof or supporting documents, but he was convinced his brother was innocent. Mathieu was received politely into office after office. Yet belief in Alfred Dreyfus's guilt was so pervasive in the country, he could not convince many people otherwise.

Even Alfred's lawyer, Demange, could not provide Mathieu

A DREYFUS.

AFFAIRE DREYFUS – LE PRISONNIER

Le Prisonnier. *A picture postcard depicting Dreyfus in prison. The ball and chain are an artistic invention.*

with any basic information. Since the trial had been held in secret, no one could divulge anything about it without facing the threat of jail. Yet slowly, Mathieu was able to piece together some details. First, the jailer Forzinetti, who had befriended Alfred, turned over papers which contained the detailed accusation of the crime. Other people provided snippets of information overheard from yet others.

Mathieu knew he had to keep interest in the Dreyfus case alive if ever he were to see his brother free again. He hired a brilliant young writer, Bernard Lazare, who himself doubted Dreyfus's guilt, to write a stirring pamphlet and then waited for the right moment to release it.

An opportunity was not long in coming. In early September 1896, a news report appeared in a small English newspaper detailing the successful escape of Alfred Dreyfus from Devil's Island. The facts were clear—even the name of the ship, the *Non-Pareil,* and its captain, a man named Hunter, were known. Quickly the report was reprinted by one of London's leading newspapers, the *London Daily Chronicle,* and then, with great fanfare, by the French press. The case of the French traitor had received coverage not only in France, but abroad. No rumor was too unimportant to share. The notorious anti-Semitic newspaper, *La Libre Parole,* complained about the existence of a "Jewish syndicate" which was plotting to free Dreyfus. The paper even printed an exclusive interview with Captain Hunter, the man who had spirited Dreyfus to freedom.

The story of the escape captivated all of France. Unfortunately, there was not a bit of truth to it. There never was even an attempted escape and there certainly was no Captain Hunter. The story was invented by Mathieu solely as a publicity gimmick and planted in the English press to keep the Dreyfus case in the public mind. In some ways, the results were more than its inventor ever imagined.

Frightened government officials scurried about trying to figure out what had happened. Although prison authorities quickly assured Paris by cable that Dreyfus had not escaped, the colonial minister, André Lebon, was nervous. If Dreyfus had really escaped, the resulting scandal would topple the government. The minister sent forceful instructions to the governor of French Guiana to build a double wall around the prisoner's hut. Until that wall was completed, Dreyfus was to be confined in his hut during the day and shackled into his bed each night.

Not only was being shackled a new and inhuman punishment for Dreyfus, it was also illegal under French penal law. It required the prisoner's legs to be placed in iron cuffs permanently mounted at the foot of his bed. Thus, from early evening until the next morning, Dreyfus was immovably secured on the bed in the stifling heat while the iron cuffs cut painfully into his skin.

By September 10, he had reached a low point. "I am so utterly weary, so broken down in body and soul, that to-day I stop my diary, not being able to foresee how long my strength will hold out, or what day my brain will succumb under the weight of so great a burden."

For twenty-four agonizing nights Dreyfus endured this added punishment. The prison commandant, a fair man trying to obey orders, visited to explain the stringent security measures. He left Devil's Island moved by what he had seen and immediately wrote a strong objection to Paris. The response from his superiors was to relieve him of duty and replace him with a cruel and vindictive penal officer, Deniel, who instituted harsher rules for the prisoner.

When the wall was finally completed and Dreyfus could again go outdoors he found that the new fence completely restricted his view of the sea. In addition, new security regulations prevented him from receiving further books and original letters from Lucie. From now on he could only receive copies of letters from his wife to ensure that no secret writing was hidden on the paper. The new rules also did not allow him to speak to his guards. He was more isolated than ever.

But Mathieu's intentions to publicize his brother's plight also had a positive result. Seeing a need to keep public opinion fixed against Dreyfus, someone within the General Staff, later assumed to be either Major du Paty or Major Henry, wrote two articles which appeared in the newspaper *L'Éclair*. The first, on September 9, simply restated the army's position on Dreyfus and hinted at evidence which existed to support his guilt. In the second article, on September 14, the writer referred to a secret file which had provided the trial judges with the evidence of guilt. He even quoted from one of the forged documents, "This Dreyfus animal is decidedly becoming too demanding."

For most people who read the article, the information only strengthened their belief in Dreyfus's guilt. But a few, learning for the first time of the secret file presented to the judges, realized that an illegal act had taken place in 1894. Even if Dreyfus were guilty, he was still entitled to his legal rights. While the army thought this admission would end public discussion of the case once and for all, the opposite reaction resulted.

On September 10, 1896, Lucie, with the help of the lawyer Demange, presented the president of the Chamber of Deputies, the lower house of the French parliament, with a formal request for Alfred's retrial. The appeal was reprinted in the newspapers. Lucie argued that news of the secret documents proved that illegal evidence, not shown to Dreyfus or his lawyer as the law required, had been used to influence the judges.

Early in November, the booklet Bernard Lazare had been working on for over a year, *Une Erreur Judiciaire* (A judicial error), was finally released with copies sent to every member of the Chamber of Deputies. A few days later, on November 10, the newspaper *Le Matin* printed a copy of the bordereau, the document which originally led to Dreyfus's arrest. Apparently, the document was sold to the newspaper by one of the handwriting experts who testified at the trial. To Mathieu and the experts he turned to, there was no doubt that the bordereau was not written by Dreyfus. Gradually, a group of loyal believers in Dreyfus's innocence gathered around Mathieu and Lucie. What had seemed a lost cause just a few months earlier was now a full-blown scandal—The Dreyfus Affair.

Meanwhile, on Devil's Island, isolated and watched continuously by an armed guard, Dreyfus had no idea of what was happening back in France. While he tried to read "between the lines" of his wife's letters for any sign of hope, his daily life was reduced to a tedious, mind- and body-numbing existence. He tried to keep himself occupied by improving his English and doing mathematical exercises. Yet the unhealthy conditions under

Devil's Island. The site of Dreyfus's imprisonment, showing his hut surrounded by a tall fence. In the rear are the guard quarters and watch tower.

which he lived prevailed. "I know of no torture more nerve-wracking and more insulting to the pride than that which I suffered . . . to have two eyes full of enmity levelled at you day and night, every instant and under every condition, and never to be able to escape or defy them!"

The authorities continually expected an escape effort from the sea. So nervous were they that during the night of June 6, 1897, when a ship was sighted far at sea, warning shots were fired at it from the island. As Dreyfus opened his eyes he saw rifles pointing directly at him. There was no doubt in Dreyfus's mind that had he made even the slightest move, the guards would have shot him dead.

The camp physician was so concerned about Dreyfus and his living conditions that he insisted to the commandant that new quarters be provided for the prisoner. In August 1897, a new cabin was built for Dreyfus on higher ground. During the construction, Dreyfus was confined to his old cabin. While the new accommodations provided more living area, it was surrounded by a high stockade fence complete with a guard tower on top of which a machine gun was mounted.

The new cabin was divided into two parts: one for Dreyfus, the other for the guards who maintained their constant vigil through a grilled partition. The windows, heavily grated, prevented proper ventilation. In the rainy season, dampness seeped through the walls sometimes leaving several inches of fetid water with nowhere to drain.

The prison commandant, Deniel, issued a long list of restrictive orders for the prisoner which were posted in the cabin. Article 27 stated: "Any communication with the outside world is forbidden him. If strange guards or convicts are on the island, he is to be shut up in the hut until their departure." Article 28 ordered: "During the night, the place occupied by the convict shall be lighted inside and occupied as during the day by a guard."

Cut Off from the World

By December 1897, Dreyfus was losing hope. Speaking with the prison physician he explained: "I am feverish: I can no longer stand up. I have given up. I'm at the end of my forces, Doctor, but what I dread most is losing my mind." Unless some positive news arrived soon from France, Dreyfus was prepared "to end the suffering."

· FIVE ·

J'Accuse *(I Accuse)*

But Dreyfus is innocent! —*Colonel Picquart*

MAJOR HENRY of the Statistical Section was in a hurry to return to his dying mother in the country. For most of March 1896, he had been away from Paris. Today's trip to the city allowed just enough time to meet Madame Bastian in a church and take the paper bag she presented him back to the office of the new chief of Intelligence, Georges Picquart. Picquart was a brilliant officer with a bright future. A wounded veteran of several colonial wars, he was chosen to observe the Dreyfus trial for the General Staff. When shortly after the trial, Colonel Sandherr, then chief of Intelligence, retired because of ill health, Picquart was appointed in his place and promoted to lieutenant colonel.

Although Dreyfus was far away from the General Staff offices, he was not totally forgotten by his superiors. As Picquart assumed his new duties, the chief of staff, General de Boisdeffre, warned the new Intelligence chief. "The Dreyfus Affair is not over. It is only beginning. A new offensive by the Jews is to be feared." Speaking bluntly, the general urged Picquart to keep "strengthening the file" on Dreyfus and urged him to become familiar with the contents. Sandherr told Picquart where the "secret file" was kept.

Picquart, as usual, handed Madame Bastian's bag to Captain Lauth, who set to the painstaking job of piecing the paper scraps together. After some time, an obviously nervous Lauth returned to Picquart's office with a taped-together blue paper. It was the unique Paris telegram known as a "petit bleu." Underground pneumatic tubes connected Paris post offices. A "petit bleu" could be sent from one post office to another and then hand-delivered by messenger to a nearby address in the city within minutes. The distinctive blue scraps which made up this "petit bleu" came from Colonel Schwarzkoppen's wastebasket. It obviously was never mailed but that did not matter to French Intelligence.

"It's frightening! Could it mean there is another traitor?" asked Lauth. For the message from the German embassy was addressed simply: Monsieur le Commandant Esterhazy, 27 Rue de la Bienfaisance, Paris. The message on the reverse read: "Sir: I am awaiting first of all a more detailed explanation than that which you gave me the other day on the subject in question. Consequently I beg you to send it to me in writing that I may judge whether I can continue my relations with the firm R. or not." It was signed with the initial "C"—known by French Intelligence to be Schwarzkoppen's personal code.

Recognizing the importance of this document, Picquart first ordered Lauth to make photographs of it and then locked the original away. He wanted to make perfectly certain of the facts before reporting to his superiors. Next, he began an investigation. Who was this officer and why was a German intelligence officer writing to him?

Marie Charles Ferdinand Walsin Esterhazy was born in Paris in 1847. Although he claimed to be descended from Hun-

A satirical cartoon. The principals in the Dreyfus Affair are depicted as a Council of Ministers. (Émile Zola is seated third from left; to his right is Mathieu Dreyfus. Colonel von Schwarzkoppen is seated fourth from right; to his right is Georges Picquart. Alfred Dreyfus is seated on the far right as minister of foreign affairs.)

garian nobility and called himself "Count," he was far from being noble. The chief of army Intelligence quickly discovered that behind the impeccably tailored uniform and gentlemanly manners lurked a sleazy opportunist who frequented gambling houses and was constantly in debt. From an officer in Esterhazy's regiment Picquart heard of the Major's poor work habits and continual interest in classified artillery information not relevant to his assigned duties.

Unknown to Picquart at the time, Major Esterhazy had visited the German Embassy in July 1894 to offer his services as a spy. He was, as usual, short of cash, and desperately needed a new source of income. Colonel Schwarzkoppen was much taken with this aristocratic traitor and began utilizing his services.

Esterhazy was also not unknown to the French General Staff. He had once served with Sandherr and Henry and, even now, was bombarding army leaders with letters requesting permanent assignment to the General Staff. Picquart informed General de Boisdeffre and the minister of war, General Jean-Baptiste Billot, of the Esterhazy investigation and was told to proceed cautiously in uncovering evidence. De Boisdeffre was clear in his instructions. "I don't want another Dreyfus Affair." A guilty Esterhazy would be quietly dismissed from the army.

On August 27, two of Esterhazy's letters to General Staff officers were turned over to Lieutenant Colonel Picquart for examination. To the Intelligence chief there was something familiar about the handwriting. Searching through his desk he pulled out a copy of the bordereau which helped convict Alfred Dreyfus. Putting one of Esterhazy's letters on the desk next to the bordereau, Picquart was more than surprised. "I was terrified," he later recounted. Could this possibly be true? Was Dreyfus falsely convicted? He needed verification.

Picquart covered the dates, the signatures, and a few easily identifiable phrases and gave the letters to Captain Lauth to photograph. When he showed copies of the photograph to du Paty and the handwriting expert Bertillon, both immediately recog-

COLONEL PICQUART

Picture postcards were used for publicity by both sides in The Dreyfus Affair. This one depicts Colonel Picquart, the head of the French Intelligence Service, who played a positive role in the Affair.

nized the handwriting as being identical to that on the borde-reau. But more proof was needed.

Picquart suddenly remembered the secret file and had it brought to him from Colonel Henry's office. Reading through it, he was puzzled by the lack of evidence. There was absolutely nothing in the file on which a court should have convicted Alfred Dreyfus. "The scoundrel D—" letter, for example, did not men-tion Dreyfus's name, only the initial "D." Yet, this was the infor-mation communicated secretly to the military judges who sent Dreyfus to Devil's Island. There was no doubt in Picquart's mind that Dreyfus had been wrongly convicted.

Another incident around that time further strengthened Pic-quart's belief. A secret agent had reported to the French military attaché in Berlin that the Germans never employed Dreyfus. The only French spy working for the Germans was a decorated infan-try major, name unknown, who had reported on maneuvers held at Chalon. Esterhazy fit the description; Dreyfus did not.

Picquart reported his grave concerns to the minister of war and to General de Boisdeffre, whose only question startled the Intelligence chief. "Why was that file not destroyed as ordered?" Regaining his composure, the chief of staff directed Picquart to consult with the deputy chief, General Gonse.

Two days later Picquart related to Gonse all that he knew about Esterhazy and the obvious connection to the Dreyfus case. Gonse replied curtly, "So, we made a mistake." Then, without any mention of what might be done to correct the error, Gonse advised, "Keep the two affairs separate." That made no sense at all to Picquart. The bordereau related to both cases. Since it was obviously written by Esterhazy, it proved that Dreyfus was inno-cent and should be released from Devil's Island.

What was clear to Picquart was the determination of his superiors not to reopen the Dreyfus case. Public disclosure of the "irregularities" surrounding Dreyfus's sentence could not only undermine respect for the army but implicate General Staff offi-cers in illegal activities related to the trial.

But truth once discovered is difficult to conceal. On September 3, the fake account of Dreyfus's escape appeared in the *London Daily Chronicle*. Mathieu's goal of increasing public interest in his brother's case succeeded. Rumors existed about the upcoming release of a dramatic pamphlet about the Affair and a member of the Chamber of Deputies, Castelin, announced that he would openly question the government about Dreyfus when parliament reopened.

Picquart knew it was only a matter of time before Mathieu Dreyfus and his supporters stumbled upon the truth. It is better, Picquart argued with his superiors, to take the offensive and deal with the truth while the army still had control over the facts. His advice fell upon deaf ears, at least in public. "Prudence! Prudence!" Gonse told him.

When the September 9 and 14 articles appeared in *L'Éclair* making knowledge of the secret file public, Picquart was irritated. The next day, he returned to General Gonse to demand an explanation. "What concern is it of yours if that Jew remains on Devil's Island?" the general asked.

"But Dreyfus is innocent," responded Picquart.

"That is a case we cannot reopen. Generals Mercier and Saussier are involved," Gonse emphasized, and then added, "If you say nothing, no one will ever know."

Picquart, unable to control his anger, blurted out, "What you say is abominable, General. I do not know what I shall do, but in any event, I shall not carry this secret with me to the grave." At that, Picquart stormed out of the room.

To Major Henry, Picquart's obsession with the Dreyfus case signaled a need to add anti-Dreyfus documents to the file while, at the same time, discrediting the Intelligence chief. The honor of the army had to be protected at any cost.

Finding a letter written by Panizzardi, the Italian military attaché in Paris, to Schwarzkoppen, the German attaché, Henry had an idea. On Sunday, November 1, 1896, with his wife at his side, the major began a delicate task. He cut off the top greeting section and the bottom signature section, found some identical paper and matching pencil and created his own letter by imitating Panizzardi's handwriting. When he concluded, he tore all three sections into small pieces then taped them together again to make it look like one of Madame Bastian's finds. The forged body of the letter stated: "If they request any new explanations at Rome, I shall say that I never had any dealings with this Jew."

On November 2, Henry took his "find" to Gonse and then to de Boisdeffre. Both generals automatically accepted its authenticity and gleefully brought the new evidence to Minister Billot, who declared it positive proof of Dreyfus's guilt. No one looked carefully at the document to notice that the paper on which the middle part of the document was written differed slightly from the paper on which the heading and signature were written. The colors were slightly off. Only Picquart was not persuaded by the "coincidence" of this "find" and expressed his doubts to General Gonse. Gonse only replied, "Whatever a minister tells me, I always believe it."

Bernard Lazare's long-awaited pamphlet reached the streets a few days later. Included were the contents of the bordereau and the information that the "scoundrel D—" letter did not refer to Dreyfus by name.

On November 10, *Le Matin* reproduced the copy of the bordereau in its original handwriting. To the Dreyfus supporters this was the important break they needed. They reproduced and distributed copies of the bordereau throughout the country in the hope that someone would recognize the handwriting. The General Staff was in an uproar and suspected Lieutenant Colonel Picquart of leaking secret information. It was clear to Gonse that Picquart posed a danger to the army. The Intelligence chief had to be removed from the scene.

The minister of war called Picquart to his office and ordered him to undertake an unusual temporary mission to survey intelligence services along France's eastern border. Picquart set out on this strange mission on November 16. His travels would take him to the French countryside, then to the port of Marseille, and ultimately across the Mediterranean to Algeria and Tunisia.

With Picquart gone, Major Henry assumed the position of acting Intelligence chief. He continued to "create" additional documents for the Dreyfus file. One document was based on a real telegram Schwarzkoppen had sent to Berlin stating that he knew nothing of Dreyfus. When Henry finished with it, the telegram read that indeed Schwarzkoppen was in contact with Dreyfus. In another letter Schwarzkoppen reported that "P— has brought me a lot of interesting things." Henry's doctored version changed the "P" to "D." There was even a letter purported to be written by Dreyfus to the ruler of Germany, the Kaiser. No one on the General Staff questioned the sudden "lucky" appearance of these incriminating documents. General Gonse proudly showed a few to Major du Paty. "Some of them strike me as suspicious," the major cautiously remarked. Later, to Major Henry, du Paty was more blunt. "Henry, take care. Your papers have a bad smell about them."

Henry also began to focus on his traveling boss. First, he sent Picquart letters of support and loyalty. At the same time, he began intercepting all personal mail sent to Picquart through headquarters. When a female friend of Picquart sent an innocent letter, playfully signed "Speranza," Henry set to work and produced a note over the same signature that seemed to involve Picquart with a "Jewish syndicate" to free Dreyfus. After Billot was shown the altered note, he became convinced of Picquart's involvement and issued orders for the intelligence chief to continue traveling on extended assignment. Picquart abruptly found himself attached to the Fourth Regiment of Sharpshooters stationed at a remote desert fort in far-off Tunisia.

Four months after he began his "inspection tour," Picquart returned to Paris on a short leave. It did not take him long to realize how he had been plotted against at headquarters. The minister of war, Billot, who had originally sent him on this special mission, would not even see him.

Shortly after his return to Tunisia, Picquart fell off a horse. He was not injured, but the accident forced him to think seriously about his position. He remembered the threat he made to General Gonse not to take the secret of the Dreyfus Affair to the grave. Picquart wrote an addition to his will in the form of a sealed letter to be delivered upon his death to the president of France. In it, he laid out all the details he had proving Dreyfus's innocence and Esterhazy's guilt. Should any harm befall him, his threat to General Gonse would be fulfilled.

The outwardly friendly correspondence between Picquart, far off in the desert, and Henry, at General Staff headquarters, changed dramatically in May 1897. Picquart, realizing he was in endless exile, wrote Henry that he was upset with all the "lies and mysteries." Henry, after consulting with General Gonse, responded rudely by accusing Picquart, his superior officer, of illegal acts. "Our inquiry has not yet been able to determine where, how and to whom the word 'lies' should be applied." Picquart now clearly understood there was a plot against him. But his loyalty to the army limited his ability to effectively fight back.

In June, Picquart arranged for a short leave in Paris where he met with his old friend and lawyer, Louis Leblois. He gave Leblois the sealed addition to the will and confided in him what he knew of the Dreyfus case and of Esterhazy's guilt. Picquart told the lawyer to keep the information secret. If absolutely necessary, the information could be given to the government but certainly not to the Dreyfus family. In any event, Picquart's identity must be concealed.

Picquart returned to Tunisia certain that if he were killed, his incredible secret would not accompany him to the grave. Not that the army didn't try to arrange Picquart's removal from the scene. Shortly after his return to Tunisia, orders from Paris directed Picquart to the battlefront where it was hoped a stray bullet would hit the trouble-making colonel. But the general on the scene saw through the plot and had the orders changed.

While Picquart may have been relieved, Leblois was troubled. The information confided to him was explosive. He couldn't just ignore it. A few days later Leblois was at a dinner party. During the evening, he could not help overhearing the dinner conversation of another guest, the elderly vice president of the Senate, Auguste Scheurer-Kestner. Scheurer-Kestner, although not thoroughly convinced of Alfred Dreyfus's innocence, was one of the few leaders in France at least willing to listen to Mathieu Dreyfus's pleas.

Leblois arranged a private meeting for later that week. Swearing Scheurer-Kestner to absolute confidentiality, Leblois told the senator all he knew. Scheurer-Kestner was speechless. Bound by a promise not to divulge either Picquart's or Esterhazy's name, the senator began to speak to everyone he met about Dreyfus's innocence. The General Staff, aware of the senator's actions, began to look for ways to discredit both him and his new cause.

Scheurer-Kestner was assured by his old friend General Billot, the minister of war, that Dreyfus was certainly guilty based on available secret documents transmitted by General Gonse (and manufactured by Major Henry). Listening to everything the senator had to say, the general convinced Scheurer-Kestner not to do anything further without discussing it with him first. In the meantime, the general promised to look further into the matter. The senator, suspecting nothing and trusting his old friend, readily agreed. The next day, Scheurer-Kestner was astonished to read an account of his private meeting with Billot in the newspaper. This was the beginning of a public campaign against the venerable and honorable senator.

Aware that Esterhazy was the target of those fighting for a review of the Dreyfus case, the General Staff sought to diffuse the "plot of the Jewish syndicate" to substitute Esterhazy for Dreyfus. There was fear that Esterhazy, under the pressure of public accusation, might do something dangerous or even commit suicide. Somehow, Esterhazy, who was "temporarily retired" on August 17, 1897, had to be warned.

An anonymous letter (actually written by Major Henry with help from his wife) signed simply, "Esperance," was sent to Esterhazy on October 18, 1897, at his country home. It warned that the Dreyfus family was about to accuse him of treason based on information provided them by Colonel Picquart. "It is up to you to defend your name and the honor of your children. Act quickly . . ." A shaken Esterhazy, unsure of what to do, returned to Paris. There, on the morning of October 22, Gribelin, the General Staff archivist, disguised in a pair of blue-tinted glasses, delivered a message at the house where Esterhazy was staying. The message directed Esterhazy to appear that evening at Montsouris Park for a meeting with an "important person."

Before going to the park, Esterhazy, afraid that his arrest was imminent, stopped at the German Embassy with a hasty plan to remove himself from further suspicion. He pleaded with Colonel Schwarzkoppen to send a letter to Madame Dreyfus informing her that her husband had indeed been a German spy. When Schwarzkoppen refused, Esterhazy ranted and raved dramatically and even drew a pistol to threaten suicide. The German attaché ordered Esterhazy thrown out of the embassy.

At the park, Esterhazy was approached by a gentleman wearing civilian dress and dark glasses. "I am Colonel du Paty de Clam of the army General Staff," the disguised man announced. "And you have only to do what I tell you." Esterhazy, much relieved, replied simply, "This is sufficient, my Colonel: You can count on my absolute obedience." The army of France had joined forces with a German spy to combat the truth.

Following the meeting, Esterhazy again stopped at the German Embassy. In a gloating voice, he calmly informed Schwarzkoppen there was now nothing to worry about. The military attaché was not convinced. On November 2, Schwarzkoppen, at his own request, was relieved of his position and recalled to Berlin. Interestingly, when he appeared a week later before Félix Faure, the president of France, to bid his official farewell, Schwarzkoppen drew the French leader aside and whispered, "I have never known Dreyfus."

Esterhazy received daily instructions and news from either du Paty, Gribelin, or Henry. When army agents reported that Senator Scheurer-Kestner had visited with the French president, du Paty, in an effort to diffuse whatever was said at the meeting, helped Esterhazy compose a letter to President Faure. In it, Esterhazy threatened to release the copy of a document, allegedly stolen by Colonel Picquart from a foreign embassy, which proved Esterhazy's innocence. The letter, Esterhazy related, was passed to him by an unknown "veiled lady." Release of the letter, he further warned, could seriously damage France's relations with the unnamed country.

To direct additional guilt at Picquart, a strange telegram was sent to Tunisia asking his superior officer to determine if, perchance, Picquart had ever been "robbed" by a veiled lady of a document from a foreign embassy.

Esterhazy, emboldened by his support from the General Staff, cloaked himself in a mantle of outraged innocence. He sent two more letters to the president, threatening to reveal compromising documents which could lead to the downfall of the government. He even had the nerve to write a letter to Picquart in which he professed shock at Picquart's attempts to implicate him. "It is unthinkable that you avoid a clear explanation."

Meanwhile Picquart received two very strange telegrams. The first, mysteriously signed "Speranza," warned, "Everything is discovered." The second, signed "Blanche," went further. "We have proof that the bleu was forged by Georges." Both telegrams, as intended by the sender, Henry, now a lieutenant colonel, were intercepted by counterintelligence in Paris and copies passed on to the minister of war, General Billot. To the officers it was further "evidence" that Picquart was implicated in a secret plot.

J'Accuse (I Accuse)

While Esterhazy felt safe because of his highly placed friends, others were beginning to chip away at his invincibility. On November 7, 1897, a Jewish stockbroker, de Castro, strolling through the streets of Paris, picked up a facsimile of the bordereau, one of thousands printed by Mathieu Dreyfus and distributed all over the city. Surprisingly, de Castro was the first to recognize the handwriting. It belonged to an army officer who owed him money—Major Ferdinand Walsin Esterhazy. De Castro visited Mathieu with the news. Now, the Dreyfus family knew what the army knew: Esterhazy wrote the bordereau.

Mathieu Dreyfus arranged a meeting with Senator Scheurer-Kestner. "It is Esterhazy!" Mathieu triumphantly announced. The senator, sworn by Leblois to absolute secrecy as to the identity of the bordereau's writer, finally breathed a sigh of relief and responded, "Yes, he's the man."

On November 14, an article appeared in *Le Figaro* describing the known facts of the case. Although Esterhazy's name was not directly mentioned, details about him appeared in the article. The army officers were nervous. The next day, with du Paty's coaching, Esterhazy wrote an article under the byline "Dixi" in *La Libre Parole*. In it Esterhazy explained that the person mentioned in the *Le Figaro* article was framed by Picquart and the supporters of Dreyfus. As to the handwriting, the article explained that Dreyfus had merely imitated the handwriting of that officer who was about to be falsely accused.

A few days later, Mathieu wrote to General Billot, officially accusing Esterhazy and demanding justice for Alfred. "I have the honor to inform you that the author of that document is Count Walsin Esterhazy. . . ." A copy of the letter was published in *Le Figaro*. This was a challenge the army could not ignore. Now, there had to be an official investigation.

Esterhazy was quick to respond. In a newspaper interview, his self-serving explanations confused the facts enough to weaken Mathieu's accusation. The visits to Schwarzkoppen were merely social, he explained: the military attaché was an old family friend.

As to the handwriting on the bordereau, Esterhazy simply could not explain the coincidence. "While the general aspect of writing is not mine . . . there are some words which seem absolutely to be written by my pen." Professing innocence, Esterhazy himself requested an investigation.

Backed into a corner, General Billot had no alternative but to order an army inquiry. Speaking in the Chamber of Deputies, Billot said, "As the guardian of the honor of the army, I shall not fail to do my duty." He appointed General Georges de Pellieux to investigate the charges against Esterhazy. Under no circumstances, however, was he to introduce into his investigation any mention of the bordereau or the "petit bleu." In other words, there could be no connection made between the Dreyfus case and the charges against Esterhazy.

Picquart was finally called back from Tunisia to be questioned by de Pellieux. The investigation's outcome was a foregone conclusion. Esterhazy, although an unsavory officer, could not be suspected of treason. After sifting through the limited testimony, the investigator came up with an illogical conclusion, "Picquart seems guilty."

No sooner had the General Staff congratulated itself, when another unexpected bombshell exploded. The November 28 issue of *Le Figaro* published copies of letters sent thirteen years earlier by Esterhazy to a lover, Madame de Boulancy, who now spitefully released them to the press. The letters, outrageously anti-French, showed Esterhazy as less than patriotic. In one letter he wrote, "These people [the French] are not worth the bullets needed to kill them. . . ." In another, he wrote, "The Germans will put all these people in their rightful places before long. . . ." The famous "Uhlan letter" was widely reprinted. In it Esterhazy wrote, "If someone were to come tell me this evening that I would be killed tomorrow as a Uhlan [German] captain killing Frenchmen with my sword, I would certainly be happy."

While Esterhazy panicked, his supporters in the army and the press, deeply involved in protecting him, loudly accused the

"Jewish syndicate" of skillful forgery and dirty tricks to embarrass the army. Most French citizens accepted that explanation and continued to support the army. Only a few voices were heard in dissent. The publisher of *L'Aurore* wondered, "Who is protecting Esterhazy?" On December 3, General de Pellieux issued a second report clearing Esterhazy of wrongdoing.

In spite of this, the cloud of suspicion would not go away. Newspaper stories continued to fuel the fire. Rumors and observations abounded, many created by Esterhazy himself, as he continued to give interviews in which he contradicted himself. While enough doubts now existed for a review of the Dreyfus case, the army was steadfast in its defense of the shady nobleman. Yet a third investigation reached the same conclusion as the previous two.

Prime Minister Jules Meline, aware of the strong pro-army feelings in the nation, spoke dramatically before the Chamber of Deputies in support of the army. He alluded to "secret documents" which unquestionably proved Dreyfus's guilt and pointed to the recently completed "meticulous" investigations which cleared Esterhazy of any wrongdoing. Then, to the cheers of the assembled deputies he stated, "There is no Dreyfus Affair."

Encouraged by the strength of his support, Esterhazy returned to his old ways. Taking on the appearance of a wrongfully maligned officer, he wrote to General de Pellieux, "As an innocent man, the torture I have been enduring . . . is superhuman." Then, as if to make it perfectly clear that he was a man in search of justice, he made a demand which he hoped would put an end to all the speculation about him. "As an officer accused of high treason, I have a right to a court-martial."

To du Paty, Count Esterhazy threatened public release of incriminating documents unless he were totally acquitted on all charges. Du Paty, suitably frustrated with the man he had broken the law to protect, loudly complained to his superiors, "This is a case of blackmail! I shall become the victim of my own good nature—I who am innocent!"

Political cartoons were widely used in newspapers to express political views of the Affair.

The court-martial opened on January 10, 1898. The trial attracted great public attention in France and abroad. In New York and London it received front-page status. Present were the few Dreyfus supporters like Lieutenant Colonel Picquart and Senator Scheurer-Kestner. Lucie and Mathieu Dreyfus were also in the courtroom, along with their lawyers. With the first part of the trial open to the public, the room was filled with military and civilian onlookers who considered Esterhazy a public hero. From the beginning it was clear that the judges would in no way allow the Dreyfus case to be revived in this courtroom.

In preparing the case, the army found handwriting experts who were influenced to conclude that the bordereau was not written by Esterhazy, the "petit bleu" was a forgery, and Madame de Boulancy's love letters could have been written by someone other than Esterhazy. With the handwriting evidence neutralized, the witnesses who followed could only present their personal opinions, which the court obviously discounted. All Scheurer-Kestner could do was to say, "I cannot say the bordereau was written by Major Esterhazy, but I affirm that the writing has a greater resemblance to Major Esterhazy's than to that of Dreyfus."

Mathieu Dreyfus stated, in contradiction of the testimony of the handwriting experts, that it was only "necessary to compare the bordereau and Major Esterhazy's handwriting in order to be convinced that they were identical."

When it was time for Colonel Picquart's testimony, the presiding judge declared the trial secret and ordered all observers from the courtroom. So harshly was Picquart treated during his testimony that one of the judges was overheard to say, "I see that the real accused is Colonel Picquart!" Indeed, the next day, after the court announced its unanimous acquittal of Esterhazy, Picquart was imprisoned to await his arraignment.

The news of Esterhazy's acquittal was received with tumultuous enthusiasm by the crowds waiting outside the court. As Esterhazy left, his supporters went wild with joy. Soldiers saluted, civilians pushed closer to touch him. They marched through the streets mingling their cheers and applause with the now familiar cries of "Death to the Jews! Long live the army!"

In the few months before the trial the number of Dreyfus supporters had been steadily increasing. Largely drawn from the ranks of the intellectuals—writers, professors, artists—they strongly believed in Dreyfus's innocence. News of the Esterhazy acquittal and the sight of rampant anti-Semitism drove one of this group of Dreyfusards, as the supporters were called, into action. In a heated rage, the noted French writer, Émile Zola, sat down at his desk and wrote all night. Zola's novels were widely read in France and, in translation, abroad. He had expressed his opposition to anti-Semitism in earlier newspaper articles, but never with such precise fury.

The next morning his words appeared in the newspaper

Émile Zola, whose article, J'accuse, *electrified the world.*

L'Aurore in the form of an open letter to the president of France, Félix Faure. The paper, which normally sold 30,000 copies a day, sold 300,000 on that day, January 13, 1898.

"*J'accuse!*" (I accuse!) The words struck at the heart of France. After presenting an impassioned review of the Dreyfus case, Zola concluded with a series of accusations against the army and the government. The army knew Dreyfus was innocent, he charged. They were only using Dreyfus to cover up a national scandal.

These excerpts from the letter show the intensity of feeling that was felt by everyone who read it.

J'Accuse (I Accuse)

I accuse Lieutenant-Colonel du Paty de Clam of having been the diabolical artisan of the judicial error . . .

I accuse General Mercier of having been an accomplice . . .

I accuse General de Boisdeffre and General Gonse of being guilty of the same crime . . .

I accuse the three handwriting experts . . . of having composed deceitful and fraudulent reports, unless a medical examination declares them to be stricken with an impairment of vision or judgment.

I accuse the offices of War of having conducted in the press, . . . an abominable campaign designed to mislead public opinion and to conceal their wrongdoing.

Finally, I accuse the first Court-Martial of having violated the law in convicting a defendant on the basis of a document kept secret, and I accuse the second Court-Martial of having covered up that illegality on command by committing in turn the juridical crime of knowingly acquitting a guilty man.

The amazing letter ended in a challenge. "I have only one passion, that for seeing the light, in the name of humanity which has so suffered and which is entitled to happiness. My fiery protest is but the cry of my soul. Let me be brought then before a criminal court and let the inquiry be held in the light of day!"

· SIX ·

A Network of Lies

I acted in the best interest of my country. —*Major Henry*

REACTION to Zola's letter was swift and predictable. Outside of France, newspapers greeted it with joy and satisfaction. Writing in the *New York Herald,* Mark Twain said, "I am penetrated with the most profound respect for Zola." Thousands of supporting letters and telegrams reached Zola from around the world.

In contrast, police in France were stationed around Zola's house to keep angry student mobs from attacking. The crowds had to be content with rock throwing and shouting, "Death to Zola! Death to the Jews! Long live the army!" Elsewhere in France, street mobs rioted against Jews and Jewish shops. Even in towns where no Jews lived, there were patriotic demonstrations.

The government was unsure of how to handle Zola's attack. While some suggested a low-key response to avoid dredging up the Dreyfus case, most felt strongly that the embarrassing accusations had to be decisively answered. At a debate in the Chamber of Deputies, the minister of war, reacting to the applause of the legislators, hastily promised legal action against Zola.

Examining options, the cabinet found a way to prosecute Zola without reopening the Dreyfus and Esterhazy trials. Zola and the publisher of *L'Aurore* would be charged with criminal libel on only one narrow point in the *J'accuse* letter, the section in which the court-martial was accused of "acting on orders" to find Esterhazy not guilty. While Zola protested the limitations, he urged his lawyer to do everything possible to focus on Dreyfus and Esterhazy.

The trial of Émile Zola opened on February 7, 1898, to great public interest. Outside the Palais de Justice, mobs supporting the army demonstrated continuously. Violence against the few Zola supporters who dared show their faces was common. Inside, the courtroom was packed with vocal army supporters including military officers, journalists, and ill-mannered rabble-rousers from the Anti-Semitic League who were not afraid to show their feelings. The jury, composed of ordinary people—shopkeepers, small businessmen, artisans—were wide-eyed at the celebrities who passed before them. Nearly two hundred witnesses were ready to be heard, including judges in the Esterhazy trial and those officers closest to the Affair such as Mercier, Billot, Picquart, and de Pellieux.

From the beginning it was clear that Judge Delegorgue would not allow the lawyers and witnesses to stray into areas not specifically covered in the charge. "The question is out of order!" he thundered whenever a pro-Zola witness tried to get in a word about the Dreyfus or Esterhazy trials.

Zola's lawyer, Fernand Labori, and Albert Clemenceau, representing his brother, Georges, publisher of *L'Aurore,* did their best to get around the judge's strict guidelines. Their goal was to get onto the official court record any information of the illegalities surrounding Dreyfus's trial in 1894. With Dreyfus's attorney, Demange, in the witness box, Clemenceau claimed the first victory.

"Wasn't it a judge of the military court who affirmed that secret proofs existed?" he hurriedly asked. Since the end of the 1894 trial, widespread gossip by the judges revealed the existence of secret documents. Before the judge could yell, "Out of order!" the witness answered, "Yes, of course." The protective wall had been cracked and the information about secret documents was on the official court record.

The trial was more theatrical than judicial. The courtroom crowd alternately cheered the anti-Dreyfus witnesses and booed those who were pro. When Mathieu Dreyfus testified, some in the audience audibly snickered. One after another, the nation's military leaders appeared. Their basic message was the same. The army did nothing wrong and must be believed, not questioned.

General de Pellieux had previously conducted a whitewash investigation of Esterhazy for the army. When his turn came to testify, the general, impatient with his colleagues' vague words, dropped a verbal bombshell. With great relish he told the court of a letter from the Italian military attaché to the German attaché which absolutely proved the guilt of Alfred Dreyfus. He even quoted the letter from memory. "Never reveal the dealings we had with this Jew." He, of course, was quoting the "Henry forgery."

Labori, recognizing the witness's admission as an embarrassment for the army, jumped from his seat demanding, "Let's see the document." General Gonse, sitting nervously in the audience, attempted to sidetrack his colleague's testimony. "The army is not afraid to reveal the truth but there is great need for caution. The proofs . . . cannot be disclosed in public." De Pellieux, now further enraged by the timidity of his colleague, ordered someone to fetch General de Boisdeffre by cab. "And there are other documents as General de Boisdeffre will tell you when he gets here." The unfortunate de Pellieux did not know the letter was a forgery. As the court adjourned for the day, the chanting intensified from the mob in the street, "Death to the Jews! Death to the Jews!"

General de Boisdeffre appeared the next day. "I shall be brief. I confirm that all the facts made by General de Pellieux in his deposition are exact and authentic." Labori, making a point for the official record, noted that the documents themselves were never produced for the court to see. Then, adding that national security was at stake, the general left the witness stand to applause saying, "I have nothing more to add." The message to all was clear. To doubt a document certified accurate by the army was the same as doubting the army itself.

That did not keep Colonel Picquart from telling the court, "That document is a forgery." General Gonse, disgusted at the officer's impudence, rose angrily from his seat. "The document is authentic but I have no right to say anything more," he emphatically stated. Then, to further discredit Picquart, General de Pellieux commented loudly to those sitting near him how odd it was that a gentleman wearing the uniform of a French soldier could accuse three loyal army generals of using forged documents. Then, turning to the jury the general added, "If the chiefs of the army are to be discredited in the eyes of the soldiers, your sons, gentlemen, will be led to the slaughter." The officers in the courtroom rose and applauded.

It was then Colonel Henry's turn to discredit Picquart. He testified that he saw Picquart show a classified military document to his lawyer, Leblois, a civilian. When Picquart countered that charge by showing that it was not physically possible for Henry to have seen any such event, Henry backed down and admitted that perhaps he had not actually witnessed the specific deed. Then, the rage which had been building up inside him erupted. Banging on the witness stand with his hand, Henry looked directly at Picquart and screamed, "I maintain that Picquart is a liar!" The usually calm and composed Picquart, his honor questioned, responded with contempt, "I am an honest man and I have done my duty."

When the trial was over, Picquart challenged Henry to a duel. The men faced each other on the field of honor on March 5. While Colonel Henry was lightly wounded in the wrist and arm, it was Picquart who was really punished for his stubborn insistence on honoring the truth. On February 26, 1898, Picquart was officially discharged from the army without a pension.

The trial, which lasted two weeks, was not without comic relief. Bertillon, the handwriting expert, completely confused and amused all who heard his convoluted and illogical testimony. Esterhazy, whose guilt was at the heart of the trial, confounded the defense lawyers by announcing, "I shall answer nothing they ask me." The ploy did not work. As Esterhazy stood silent in the witness box, lawyers posed "loaded" questions, which although unanswered, still got important facts into the official court records. When he was finally excused, Esterhazy received a standing ovation. People hugged and kissed him as he left the building. "Long live the victim of the Jews!" they shouted.

As the trial neared a close, public reaction grew more intense. Violent incidents arose as the entire country awaited the verdict. On February 22, Zola dramatically addressed the court. "Dreyfus is innocent," he exclaimed. "I swear it." The following day the jury retired to reach a verdict. It did not take long: they returned thirty-five minutes later. Guilty! The two defendants were each fined 3,000 francs and sentenced to prison—Zola for one year, the publisher for four months.

The officers in the courtroom embraced each other and shouted for joy. Zola, surrounded by a protective shield of supporters, left to the jeers of a menacing crowd. "Long live the army! Death to Zola! Death to the Jews!" Later, one of Zola's friends said, "If Zola had been acquitted, not one of us would have come out alive."

Throughout France ugly demonstrations erupted against Jews. People ran through the streets proclaiming the greatness of the army. They saw Zola's guilty verdict as a victory for France. Dreyfus supporters at first thought their cause over as anti-Semitic acts of violence, boycotts of Jewish businesses, and calls to throw all Jews out of France were present everywhere. The world looked on with disbelief as all reason seemed to have left the French mind.

But Mathieu Dreyfus was not totally dismayed. If nothing else, the Zola trial succeeded in placing upon the official court record all that was known about his brother's innocence, Esterhazy's guilt, and the army's illegal involvement. Although it was hard to tell from the demonstrations in the streets, public opinion had also been affected for the cause of justice. Although mobs of army supporters seemed to rule the streets, the growing number of people convinced of Dreyfus's innocence ensured that the case could not be forgotten.

Zola appealed his conviction on a technicality. The High Court agreed and a new trial was ordered which would focus on an even narrower aspect of the *J'accuse* letter. Before that trial could open on July 18, 1898, Émile Zola, convinced he would not have a fair trial, sadly left France for exile in England.

During all the tumult surrounding the Zola trial, the Jews of France tried to keep a low profile. They feared calling attention to themselves by having their loyalty to France questioned. This did not stop the political right and Church affiliated groups from waging a continuous campaign of hate. The newspaper of the Catholic Assumptionist Fathers, *La Croix,* exceeded even Drumont's *La Libre Parole* in the output of anti-Semitic frenzy.

Jews were denounced as evil influences on French society. Anti-Jewish songs, some written by priests, appeared along with cartoons in which Jews were stereotypically depicted in the most vulgar ways. When Prime Minister Meline addressed the Chamber of Deputies just after the Zola trial, he blamed the Jews for creating the anti-Semitism. "The Jews who foolishly unloosed this prepared campaign of hatred brought down upon themselves a century of intolerance."

In the next national election held in May 1898, the government changed hands. No politician who actively supported Dreyfus was reelected to the Chamber of Deputies. The new prime minister was Henri Brisson, a loyal supporter of the French Republic. He appointed a new minister of war, Godefroy Cavaignac, who immediately set out to erase all lingering doubts swirling about the army by proving once and for all time that Dreyfus was guilty. He hoped to finally silence all the Dreyfus supporters in France and abroad.

To find his evidence, Cavaignac did not look any further than the thick folder on the Dreyfus case he had requested from the General Staff. Several ministry officers, including Captain Louis Cuignet, were already reviewing the contents—over three hundred mostly meaningless documents including forgeries by Major Henry. But Cavaignac, not realizing the flimsiness of the evidence, appeared before the Chamber of Deputies on July 7 to state his long-awaited proof. It was a moment he would soon regret.

The entire Chamber drew silent as the minister of war began his remarks. "I am completely certain of Dreyfus's guilt," he announced. He continued by reviewing the entire case and ended by quoting three "out of a thousand" documents which proved Dreyfus's guilt. The document which created the most reaction was the letter from Panizzardi to Schwarzkoppen referring to "dealings with this Jew" (the forgery concocted by Major Henry and his wife on November 1).

The deputies rousingly cheered the clear "proofs" of the new minister of war and voted to print Cavaignac's speech, including a copy of the Panizzardi letter, and post it publicly in each of the country's thirteen thousand communities. The speech only strengthened beliefs on both sides of the Dreyfus question. Colonel Picquart again made it known that the minister was quoting from forged documents. Dreyfus supporters knew it was only a matter of time before that fact would be more widely believed.

To close the circle of justice even tighter, Cavaignac ordered Esterhazy and Picquart arrested—Esterhazy on July 12 and Picquart on July 13—and taken to the Santé prison. A court-martial found Esterhazy guilty of improper behavior and his name was removed from the officer list. He was released from jail a month later but not before implicating Colonel du Paty in his activities. Picquart was charged with espionage, accused of passing secrets to his lawyer, Leblois. He remained in Santé prison.

On the night of August 13, 1898, the conscientious Captain Cuignet was at home reviewing documents from the Dreyfus file. It was dark and he examined the documents by lamplight. As he passed one pieced-together taped letter before the light he noticed something strange. The letter, although supposedly written on one piece of graph-like paper, actually came from two separate sheets. The color of the lines differed ever so slightly. Under normal daylight the differences were almost impossible to detect. But in the intense light of the lamp the difference was clearly visible. This was the Pannizardi letter Cavaignac had presented to the Chamber of Deputies as the ultimate "proof" of Dreyfus's guilt. Copies were now plastered on walls throughout France. Picquart was right. It was an obvious forgery.

Cavaignac was furious. It was not just the embarrassment but the realization that he had been duped by the only man who could have engineered the forgery, Colonel Hubert Henry, then on summer leave. When he returned on August 30, Henry was escorted to Cavaignac's office by General Gonse. Also present was General de Boisdeffre. Neither general knew the purpose of the meeting in advance.

At first, Henry denied any involvement with forgery, but Cavaignac interrogated the colonel without mercy. "Tell me what happened. What did you do?"

"I arranged a few sentences," was all the colonel would

admit at first. Only after continued questioning did Henry begin to explain. "My superiors were concerned and I wanted to calm them. I said to myself: Let us add a sentence that can pass as proof. . . . I acted in the best interest of my country."

"Is it not true," Cavaignac pressed the increasingly frightened colonel, "that you made up the text?" Henry, seeing the vise closing even tighter upon him, continued to deny everything. "I swear I did not," he responded. An hour after entering the room, Henry finally broke down under the relentless questioning and confessed that he had indeed forged the letter.

"So this is what happened," Cavaignac said in summary. "In 1896 you received . . . an insignificant letter: you destroyed the letter and fabricated another. Is that so?"

Henry, now visibly shaken, whispered a simple, "Yes."

Generals Gonse and de Boisdeffre, who knew of the forgery and tried to avoid the document's use in the Esterhazy trial, sat glumly throughout the questioning. As Henry was led out of the minister's office under arrest, General de Boisdeffre sat down at Cavaignac's desk and wrote out his resignation: "I have the honor to ask to be relieved of my duties."

Henry was taken to the fortress at Mont-Valérien and placed in a room in the officers' wing. A short news bulletin was issued to the press saying that Colonel Henry had confessed to writing the letter of October 1896 in which Dreyfus was named. News of the confession stunned France. General de Pellieux, upset at the role thrust upon him in the Affair, offered his resignation, which was not accepted. In one way or another, France's leading military personalities had been involved in the cover-up of the "Henry forgery." The next day, Colonel Hubert Henry killed himself in his prison room by slitting his throat with a razor.

The confession and death of Colonel Henry seemed to leave no doubt that a revision, or review, of Dreyfus's original sentence was at hand. Even the notoriously anti-Semitic newspapers like *La Libre Parole* accepted that fact while maintaining "Revi-

Esterhazy in London. *A picture postcard depicting Esterhazy, "the real traitor," in London, where he sold conflicting stories about the Affair to newspapers.*

sion Means War." The government of Prime Minister Brisson, with the exception of Cavaignac, now favored this step to finally clear the air. But rather than have the government initiate the controversial action, word was sent to Mathieu Dreyfus to make the formal request on behalf of the family. Like all other aspects of the case, revision would not come easily.

Even Esterhazy saw the handwriting on the wall. On September 1, despite the unwavering support from the army, Esterhazy shaved off his moustache, crossed the border into Belgium, and fled to England under an assumed name. There he lived out his life for the next twenty-five years, confessing his guilt from time to time to newspapers willing to pay him for his ever-changing stories.

Cavaignac, although still convinced of Dreyfus's guilt, resigned. In his place came General Zurlinden, the military governor of Paris, who began to review the Dreyfus case himself. Like

Cavaignac he also believed that Picquart, still in prison, was guilty of forging the "petit bleu" and aiding the "Jewish syndicate" in substituting Esterhazy for Dreyfus.

He wanted Picquart brought before a court-martial. If he were convicted as a forger, Picquart's testimony at a future Dreyfus trial would be valueless. At a hearing to decide if Picquart should be tried by a military court rather than a civilian one, Picquart expressed concern for his personal safety. "I want it known," he said, "should . . . Henry's razor be found in my cell, that it will have been a murder. For I would never think of suicide."

Zurlinden was not happy with the legal paperwork part of the minister of war's position and resigned within a few weeks to return to his previous position as military governor of Paris. He, in turn, was succeeded by General Chanoine. But before leaving office, Zurlinden, nettled by the accusations Esterhazy made against Colonel du Paty, had du Paty retired from the army and put on half pension as punishment.

The High Court of Appeals (Cour de Cassation) began deliberations on revision at the end of September amid much confusion both in and out of court. In the streets of Paris there were continuous demonstrations, sometimes violent, both for and against revision. The country was more divided than ever. A popular cartoon of the period by the artist Caran d'Ache showed two scenes of a family sitting down to a dignified dinner. As soon as the name of Dreyfus is mentioned, the guests begin throwing dishes and screaming at each other.

The Revisionists, as Dreyfus supporters were known, came mainly from the political left. They included supporters of the French Republic, socialists, and those committed to social justice and democracy. Arrayed against them were the anti-Revisionists, who preferred France to be ruled by a strong dictatorial system. Among them were a good number of Catholic clergy, nationalists, anti-Semites, soldiers, and monarchists.

Most active in the street fighting and demonstrations

Pageants and other public forms of entertainment honored Dreyfus and the Dreyfusard cause.

against Dreyfus were members of the Patriotic League and the Anti-Semitic League. The nationalist newspapers mounted attacks on the High Court to influence the judges' decision against a new Dreyfus trial while the Revisionists reacted to the increased involvement of the Church and the army in political life.

Prime Minister Brisson had other problems. There were violent strikes by World's Fair construction workers and railroad employees. Street demonstrations grew more violent and army troops were called out to preserve order in Paris. Everywhere there were rumors of plots against the Republic. On October 25, 1898, during a debate on revision in the Chamber of Deputies, the latest minister of war abruptly announced his resignation. Continuing the tradition of the two previous ministers, Chanoine declared that he still believed Dreyfus guilty. The rest of the cabinet resigned and the tortured government of Prime Minister Brisson ended.

President Félix Faure appointed Charles Dupuy as prime minister of yet another government. The new minister of war was Charles de Freycinet, a civilian.

Just four days later, on October 29, the Criminal Chamber of the High Court agreed there were grounds for a review of the Dreyfus case and a further investigation would begin at once. One judge said: "It is not too much to affirm that the accusation is now entirely nullified." The Dreyfusards had won the first legal round in reversing the injustice of 1894.

In early November the Court began its preliminary investigation. Witnesses were called, including all five of the previous ministers of war, each of whom proclaimed Dreyfus guilty. When the judges asked General Mercier about the secret file, he replied, "I don't think it behooves the Court to concern itself with that question." The Court, however, requested the government to turn it over.

The army, still trying to arrange for Colonel Picquart's court-martial, claimed it needed the file as evidence. After much wrangling, a compromise was reached whereby the file was hand-carried to the court each day by Captain Cuignet and returned to the ministry of war each evening. To the delight of the Revisionists it kept Picquart from a military trial in which he would have been found guilty, thereby hurting his important testimony at any upcoming Dreyfus retrial. Later, the High Court ruled that Picquart's alleged crime of revealing secret documents was indeed a civil matter thereby saving Picquart from the revenge of his former colleagues in the army.

It did not take long for the judges to realize how empty of evidence that supposedly important file was. Dozens of witnesses were called, including Major Esterhazy, who returned to France under a safe-conduct agreement. During the months of conflicting testimony and heated discussion which followed, it became clear that Dreyfus was innocent. One judge commented, "I have come to the conclusion that the bordereau was not written by Dreyfus but by Esterhazy."

In that world turned upside down, Colonel Henry, the dead and confessed forger, soon became a martyred hero. The nationalist papers explained away his actions by saying they had been committed to protect the honor and security of France. In their eyes the "patriotic forgery" was a noble and honorable act.

La Libre Parole began a fund-raising campaign for Henry's poor widow and orphan to defend the honor of "the French officer killed, murdered by the Jews." Over 25,000 people from all over the country contributed, many from church institutions and the military. The newspaper published the names of the contributors along with the hateful anti-Semitic comments many sent along with their money. One person wrote he was "training dogs to devour Jews." Another said the Jews should all be poisoned.

When the president of France, Félix Faure, died unexpectedly on February 16, 1899, the continuation of the French Republic was much in doubt. His successor was Émile Loubet, the respected president of the Senate. Some called for the re-establishment of a monarchy. Anti-Semitic and other nationalist parties readied their street thugs for action. The leader of the Patriotic League approached General de Pellieux in an effort to get the army's support to overthrow the government. The plan called for de Pellieux to lead his troops from their place in the president's funeral procession and seize the Presidential Palace. De Pellieux wisely absented himself from the funeral and the revolt ended before it could start.

In May, de Freycinet became the latest minister of war to resign. He was replaced by Camille Krantz, the minister of public works.

On May 29, 1899, the High Court finally convened to resolve the question of revision. On June 3, the long-awaited verdict of the High Court was announced amid pomp and solemnity. The court set aside the original sentence and ordered

Lucie Dreyfus at home in Paris with son Pierre and daughter Jeanne. Lithograph by Charles Paul Renouard.

Alfred Dreyfus to stand trial at a new court-martial to take place at Rennes. In the courtroom, Mathieu Dreyfus, Bernard Lazare, and other Revisionists hugged and embraced. At her nearby home, Lucie Dreyfus was overwhelmed with joy as she told her children the good news that their father was coming home.

The following day, Émile Zola returned home from England. On June 13, all charges against Colonel Picquart were dropped. After three hundred eighty-four days in jail, the honorable colonel was a free man once more.

During all the upheavals of the previous year, the man whose name was at the center of all the commotion remained unaware of the efforts to free him. His life continued amidst the mind-numbing conditions which were imposed on him by his jailers. Only in early November 1898 did he finally receive a letter from Lucie in which she informed him about her request to the government for a revision of his sentence. Dreyfus's hopes were raised a bit more when he later received an official letter telling him that the High Court had accepted the application for revision.

Only in the end of December 1898 did he receive a copy of the prosecutor's October opening speech before the High Court. Reading it, Dreyfus for the first time learned several key facts about his case: Mathieu's accusation against Esterhazy, Esterhazy's acquittal, and Henry's forgery and suicide. In spite of these disconnected facts, Dreyfus remained nearly totally ignorant of the High Court's lengthy ongoing investigation.

Beginning on November 28, Dreyfus found his living conditions slowly improving. His prisoner's food allotment was upgraded and he was allowed more freedom to move about the fortified area surrounding his hut. He could again gaze upon the ocean. As he paced to and fro he could only imagine what course the legal activity on his behalf was taking. "While my will did not weaken during these eight long months in which I was looking daily and hourly for the decision of the High Court, my physical and cerebral exhaustion grew more pronounced."

For Alfred Dreyfus, news of the High Court's final decision came from a guard who entered his cell shortly after noon on June 5, 1899, to read him the official notice.

"Please let Captain Dreyfus know immediately of this order of the High Court. The Court annuls the sentence pronounced on the 22nd of December 1894, upon Alfred Dreyfus, by the first Court-Martial of the Military Government of Paris and remands the accused party to a Court-Martial at Rennes.

"In virtue of this decision Captain Dreyfus becomes a sim ple prisoner under arrest and is restored to his rank and allowe to resume his uniform.

"The cruiser *Sfax* leaves Fort-de-France today with orders to take the prisoner from Devil's Island and bring him back to France."

On June 9, 1899, Dreyfus boarded the *Sfax*. "My joy was boundless," he later wrote. After four years and three months on Devil's Island, Alfred Dreyfus was going home.

· SEVEN ·

The Horizon Brightens

I swear again that I am innocent.
—*Alfred Dreyfus*

AFTER five years of constant suffering, the ocean voyage afforded Alfred a period of quiet relaxation. Aboard the *Sfax* he was treated according to regulations as an officer under arrest. His small cabin had bars over the portholes, and the glass door kept him visible to the constant guard outside. Twice a day he was allowed to stroll on deck to savor the fresh smell of the ocean and the refreshing sun-splashed spray of sea water. Yet, no one on board talked to him.

"Of my own story I knew nothing. I was still back in 1894 with the bordereau as the only document in the case," he later recounted. In a copy of the London *Times,* loaned to him by a kindly officer, Dreyfus read of Colonel du Paty's arrest. That news reinforced his beliefs that justice was finally at hand. With the sighting of the French coast on June 30, that dream was shattered.

After waiting an entire day on board, Dreyfus was transferred at night in a rough sea from one small ship to another. It was well after midnight when a lifeboat landed him at the small village of Port Houliguen. From there he was whisked by carriage to the railroad station at Quiberon. Armed soldiers lined the road. He arrived at the prison in Rennes the next morning at six o'clock, chilled and exhausted.

The shock of his abrupt and unceremonious arrival was softened a few hours later when he was reunited with Lucie. They were deliriously happy to hold and touch one another after the years apart, but each could not help noticing how the other had changed. Lucie's face had a concerned and hardened look; Alfred appeared dramatically aged, his hair snow white, his figure stooped and frail. He did not see the children. They were kept home to spare them from seeing their father as he now looked and to avoid disappointment if the trial did not free him. He was constantly cold even though it was July, and suffered from chills and fever. He began a diet of milk and eggs to regain his strength.

On July 3, Dreyfus met the attorneys who would represent him at the court-martial. He already knew Edgar Demange, his lawyer at the 1894 trial. New was Fernand Labori, Zola's lawyer. For the next five weeks, between visits from Lucie, Mathieu, and other relatives, Dreyfus tried to catch up on what had happened to his case during the previous five years. For the first time he learned about Picquart's relentless search for the truth and Esterhazy's role as the real spy. He was given the details about Émile Zola's bravery and Henry's suicide. With faith in his beloved army still intact, Dreyfus could only express "an overpowering pity and sorrow for that army of France which I loved."

Reaction to Dreyfus's return and upcoming trial varied. While thousands of letters and telegrams of support arrived in Rennes, nationalist newspapers shrilly called for the new court-martial to send Dreyfus back to Devil's Island.

On June 12 the government of Charles Dupuy fell. The

new cabinet was headed by René Waldeck-Rousseau, a prime minister dedicated to keeping the republican form of government alive in France. He appointed General Gaston de Gallifet as the new minister of war. To demonstrate his determination from the first, Waldeck-Rousseau clamped down on the street demonstrations and increased church political activities. For his part, de Gallifet began a shake-up of the army's senior command.

The new government was well aware of the dangers it faced from the new Dreyfus trial. If Dreyfus were found innocent, it would signal the necessity of bringing the nation's military leaders to trial for their role in the Affair. On the other hand, a guilty verdict would lift the threat of prosecution from the generals. The cry from the nationalist press was "Dreyfus or Mercier [the general who first accused Dreyfus in 1894], the court-martial will choose." All eyes were on Rennes.

Rennes was a quiet little town in Brittany not comfortable with the spectacle which suddenly engulfed it. Army patrols turned the peaceful village into an armed camp complete with the color, sound, and character of a military occupation. Journalists from around the world descended upon the town and immediately hired local boys to act as messengers. Although the best telegraphers in the country had been sent to Rennes, the small telegraph office was quickly overwhelmed by the onrush of dispatches to satisfy the international interest in the trial. The town's high school auditorium was selected as the site for the trial. It offered the largest enclosed space suitable for the crush of dignitaries and important witnesses. Official passes were needed to go anywhere near the area.

The simple residents of Rennes did not welcome the sophisticated Dreyfusards from Paris. Townspeople gathered to watch the activity and cheer the anti-Dreyfus witnesses going to and from the temporary courthouse. Accommodations were hard to find. Lucie, Mathieu, and other supporters stayed at the house of a Madame Godard.

In spite of the continued hatred surrounding him in France,

Dreyfus and his supporters remained very optimistic. After all, they reasoned, the clear decision of the High Court of Appeals made it almost automatic that he would now be freed. But they still underestimated the power of the army and its unwillingness to accept the verdict of a civilian court.

The court-martial opened on August 7, 1899. The charge against the defendant was similar to the original one he faced in 1894—delivering the documents listed in the bordereau to a foreign power. Many of the same witnesses who appeared before the Zola trial and the High Court of Appeals were scheduled to testify again, only this time before a military court. While the first court-martial lasted three days, this trial took five weeks. There were seven judges, all army officers. The chief judge, or president, was Colonel Albert Jouaust.

Court sessions were scheduled to begin in the early morning due to the unbearable midday August heat. The first session opened at seven AM as the president ordered: "Bring in the accused!" All in the courtroom rose for a look at the prisoner.

"There entered a little old man—an old man of thirty-nine who had the gait of an Egyptian mummy," wrote a reporter. The new uniform Dreyfus wore could not disguise the ordeal of the previous five years. He was thin and his skin yellow. Nonetheless he carried himself as the proud soldier he was. He walked, sat, and saluted with as much military precision as he could muster. But when he spoke, his voice was flat and undramatic.

Colonel Jouaust began by forcefully and methodically questioning Dreyfus about every aspect of the bordereau. When confronted again with the question of whether the handwriting was his, Dreyfus could control his silent anger no longer. "It is unjust to condemn an innocent man!" he cried, raising his white-gloved right hand aloft. "I swear again that I am innocent."

The next three days—August 8, 9, 10—were spent in sessions closed to reporters and the public to discuss the contents of the secret file. It was already known from previous civil court

Dreyfus Speaks *by Charles Paul Renouard, 1899. Captain Dreyfus testifies at the Rennes trial. His lawyer, Demange, sits behind him.*

testimony that the file contained much misinformation but the court-martial laboriously reviewed item after item.

As if there were not enough forgeries already in the file, Labori noticed the officer presenting the file stuff an additional document into the folder. When he demanded an explanation, the officer apologized to the court and sheepishly admitted that he was adding a document given to him by General Mercier. It turned out to be the false translation by du Paty of a message sent by Panizzardi to Rome on November 2, 1894. The original document, which conveniently disappeared, actually showed Dreyfus's innocence. The du Paty substitution, one of the documents given to the 1894 judges, had been discounted by the High Court earlier. In fact, du Paty was awaiting trial for knowingly submitting this misleading translation now brought back to life. "Captain Dreyfus is arrested. The minister of war has proof of his relations with Germany. All my precautions are taken."

The next public session was on August 12. During the five weeks of the trial there were over ninety witnesses: seventy for the government and twenty for Dreyfus. Perhaps the star witness of them all was General Mercier, recognized as the leader of the anti-Dreyfusards at Rennes.

His appearance was long awaited. Before the trial he boasted that once on the stand he would sink the Dreyfus cause by presenting a "devastating revelation." That bombshell was supposed to be a photograph of the original bordereau with a handwritten note in the margin by the German Kaiser himself. Naturally, Mercier claimed, the original was returned to Germany to avoid war. Once the trial began, the "revelation" was never brought up.

Instead, Mercier tried to convince the court that "in 1894, we were within an ace of war" with Germany. Insisting that the German Kaiser himself was involved in the espionage activities, Mercier added that "everyone at the Kaiser's castle knew the name of Dreyfus."

Throughout his testimony Mercier referred to documents, like the "scoundrel D—" letter, to prove Dreyfus's guilt: documents which the High Court had previously declared untrue. In fact, his testimony ignored the known truth and was riddled with disproven facts and rumors. These lies, however, were delivered in a soft-spoken, convincing style.

Jean Casimir-Perier, who in 1894 was president of France, sat silently fuming in the courtroom and shook his head in disagreement with everything Mercier said. At the end of the session he demanded, and received, the opportunity to respond to Mercier the next day. Aside from asserting the lack of a war threat from Germany in 1894, he wanted it also put on the record that it was Mercier who plainly told him then that "D" was none other than Dreyfus.

In a clever conclusion to his testimony, General Mercier spoke of Dreyfus. "If the slightest doubt crossed my mind I would be the first to tell you so and to say to you and to Captain Dreyfus, 'I erred in good faith and I have come to acknowledge it in all honesty and do all that is humanly possible to right the terrible wrong that was done.'" Dreyfus, who had been sitting quietly throughout Mercier's presentation, suddenly jumped up and passionately shouted at the general, "That is what you should do! It is your duty!"

General Mercier paused and coolly responded. "Well, no. My conviction has not weakened at all since 1894. It has only been strengthened." With that, Mercier withdrew, at least formally. But informally his presence was felt throughout the trial. He acted like the stage manager of an amateur play, coaching military officers and posing questions directly to witnesses whenever he felt the need.

Early on the morning of August 14, the lawyer Fernand Labori strolled casually toward the courthouse in the company of Colonel Picquart and another man. Suddenly, a shot rang out from behind. Labori could only exclaim, "Ooh, la, la!" as he fell wounded to the pavement. Picquart set out after the culprit on foot, yelling for people ahead to stop him. But the man kept running unhindered shouting, "Let me by, I just killed Dreyfus's lawyer!" He escaped.

At the courtroom, news of the shooting came almost immediately. A policeman rushed into the room to announce, "Quick, a doctor. Mr. Labori has been wounded!" There was profound shock on both sides at the horrible attack. Labori recovered and was able to return to court a week later but there was no doubt that his client's case had been damaged. Demange, Dreyfus's other lawyer, was respected and intelligent, but he lacked Labori's courtroom daring. During Labori's absence, General Mercier had become more blatantly outspoken. No one dared silence him.

The witnesses who followed added nothing new to what was already known. Their testimonies were in keeping with the French practice of allowing witnesses to pass along any statement, comment, or unrelated rumor they wished without the necessity of offering specific proofs as in American or British courts. During the court-martial much of what was heard against Dreyfus could either not be proven or was irrelevant to the specific charges of the case.

Former ministers of war Billot, Chanoine, and Zurlinden testified of their unshakable belief that Dreyfus wrote the bordereau. General de Boisdeffre shared their view. General Roget denounced Dreyfus in bitter terms, repeating all sorts of unprovable assertions.

One charge was that Esterhazy was in the employ of the Dreyfus family. Demange attempted to deflect that testimony by asking, "How do you explain the fact that Esterhazy upon several occasions wrote statements calculated to compromise the case of Dreyfus?" Roget, still unable to offer real proof, could only respond, "With Esterhazy, one can never be sure of anything. He is such an extraordinary fellow." Even the audience laughed. Later in the trial four different witnesses testified against Esterhazy, but the original lies remained on the court record.

The Dossier *by Charles Paul Renouard. At the Rennes court-martial in 1899, soldiers carry a basket of documents.*

Mrs. Henry, dressed in black, assured the court that her husband did only what was necessary "in the interest of the army." When Captain Cuignet, the discoverer of the letter forged by Henry, related more misinformation based on rumors, Dreyfus lost control and interrupted: "I cannot spend all this time listening to such lies."

Colonel Picquart's appearance made a positive impression. Dressed in civilian clothes, the man whose military career was now in ruins spoke of his original belief that Dreyfus was guilty and how a study of the documents, including the finding of the "petit bleu," made him realize that the accused captain was really innocent and that Esterhazy was guilty. Generals Gonse, Mercier, and de Pellieux all tried to refute Picquart's testimony but to no avail.

The sessions of August 25 and 26 were largely devoted to handwriting expert Alphonse Bertillon, who turned the courtroom into a classroom, complete with blackboard, charts, and papers. Now the chief of the Anthropometric Department of the Paris Prefecture of Police, Bertillon succeeded only in what he had done best at previous trials—confusing judges and spectators alike with convoluted theories. He and several other experts from the 1894 trial stated that Dreyfus authored the bordereau. A few days later their testimonies were refuted by other handwriting experts who demonstrated clearly that it was impossible for Dreyfus to have written it.

When Captain Martin Freystaetter took the stand, he addressed the issue of the secret file and its illegal use by the judges in the 1894 trial. He had been one of the judges during that trial, and he testified that Colonel Maurel, president of the court-martial, read documents from that file to the other judges. Earlier, Colonel Maurel had stated that at no time did he have access to the secret file. When Freystaetter further stated that Maurel read the Panizzardi letter to the judges, General Mercier jumped up and said, "It is a lie!" The witness responded convincingly: "I swear that what I have said is true and I have a vivid recollection of the fact that the first words were 'Captain Dreyfus is arrested.'"

General Mercier answered that he did not invent the file, Colonel Sandherr did. Labori, pointing out the absence of proof in the general's shifting testimony, said, "Colonel Sandherr is dead, Colonel Henry is dead, and Colonel du Paty de Clam won't come here."

Labori's attack did not seem to slow Mercier down. At the trial's conclusion the general verbally attacked Captain Freystaetter then pointedly reminded the judges that when they reached a verdict, the decision would be for "either Dreyfus or myself."

In spite of the groundwork laid by the defense lawyers for

Dreyfus, the verdict of the all-military jury was in doubt. The testimony so far did not focus enough on the bordereau. Labori, sensing the need for a dramatic "clincher," sent telegrams to the German Kaiser and the Italian King asking them to allow Schwarzkoppen and Panizzardi to testify at Rennes. When that request was refused, the prime minister, Waldeck-Rousseau, sent his own message to the Kaiser asking that Schwarzkoppen at least be allowed to issue a statement. The Kaiser commented sarcastically to his aides, "Am I the Kaiser of France?"

But in a concession to goodwill, the following statement of the German secretary of state appeared for all to see in the official journal of the German government for September 8: "I declare as positively as possible that there has never been any connection whatever between the French ex-Captain Dreyfus and any German agents."

On September 7 the official prosecutor, Commandant Carrière, who was overshadowed much of the time during the trial by Mercier and others, delivered his final summation. He said that although he had hoped to demonstrate Dreyfus's innocence, "this mass of witnesses who have come to give us information and personal opinions have destroyed that hope."

His arguments were filled with undocumented charges and incomplete ideas. "Esterhazy," he said, "undoubtedly served as Dreyfus's intermediary, but we have no proof of this." Continuing, he urged the judges to consider the "two categories of witnesses, those for and those against the prisoner. Weigh their importance." He concluded simply but without any substantiation, "Gentlemen, proof is everywhere. I tell you, Dreyfus is guilty!"

The next day, Demange, speaking for the defense, began an organized, well-thought-out final speech in which all the arguments against Dreyfus were analyzed and refuted. For the rest of the day and into the next session he went through the bordereau line by line to prove that Dreyfus could not have written it. He urged the judges, as military men, to "never admit as proofs the

Dreyfus at the Rennes court-martial in 1899.

hypothesis and presumptions advanced here." While his remarks were well reasoned, the presentation lacked the passion Labori would have given. "Why, you must not say a thing is possible. A judge must have proof. No doubt must rest on the conscience of a judge." Some also thought Demange showed too much deference to the judges and to the army. His closing line was, "I have confidence in you because you are all soldiers."

The last words in the trial belonged to Alfred Dreyfus: "I affirm before my country and before the army that I am innocent. My sole aim has been to save the honor of my name and the name my children bear. I have suffered five years of the most awful tortures. But, today, I am convinced that I am about to attain my desire, thanks to your honesty and justice."

With that, at three-fifteen PM on September 9, 1899, Colonel Jouaust formally declared the proceedings closed. After thirty-three sessions and nearly one hundred witnesses, the second court-martial was over. The judges and army witnesses rose as one and marched out of the hall in cadence, as if in some military parade.

Less than two hours later the judges returned. As policemen hovered around the judges' podium to prevent demonstrations, Colonel Jouaust announced the strange verdict. "The accused is guilty, but with 'extenuating circumstances.'" He was sentenced to ten years detention. Demange and Labori cried at the news.

Dreyfus, according to regulation, was not in the courtroom. Demange, unable to face the prisoner, sent Labori out to break the news. "You are condemned," Labori whispered as he clasped Dreyfus in his arms, "but you will not go back to Devil's Island."

Breaking away from the embrace, Dreyfus calmly shook hands with his lawyer and without a hint of emotion simply said, "Take care of my wife and children." The next day Dreyfus signed a formal request for an appeal before the High Court.

The court-martial judges voted five to two in favor of conviction. Yet by also citing "extenuating circumstances" they indi-

Exiting the Lycée *by Charles Paul Renouard. Dreyfus leaves the Court at Rennes as soldiers turn away in disrespect.*

cated uncertainty of their decision. In a highly unusual move, the judges met the next day and unanimously voted to request the government not to subject Dreyfus to a second humiliating degradation ceremony.

The verdict did not satisfy many people. Dreyfus supporters overseas could not believe that a court could so ignore the evidence. Anti-French demonstrations were held in cities around the world from London to New York. Mass meetings were held throughout the United States urging President William McKinley to take diplomatic action against France. The summer residents of Northeast Harbor, Maine, were so upset they sent a telegram of sympathy to Madame Dreyfus at Rennes. And, as a symbol of support, the people of Wichita, Kansas, elected a Jewish girl, Miss Sadie Joseph, as Queen of the Flower Parade at the Fall Carnival. French embassies were guarded against attacks. Efforts were begun in many countries to boycott the World's Fair scheduled to open in Paris the next year.

In France, anti-Dreyfusards rejoiced, but not fully. They thought the court had been too lenient. But General Mercier and the army were satisfied, for the guilty verdict also set them free from the threat of prosecution.

Prime Minister Waldeck-Rousseau was not happy with the decision either. He had hoped that a verdict of innocence would put an end to the national bickering. Now, he had only one course of action open—a pardon for Dreyfus. While a pardon could not substitute for a court-directed verdict of not guilty (the prisoner was still legally guilty of treason), it would allow Dreyfus to be released from prison. President Émile Loubet, like many Dreyfus supporters, wanted to set the captain free but did not favor a pardon because it did not address the issue of innocence. But he also realized that Dreyfus had suffered enough and even now was on the brink of a physical and emotional breakdown. Discussions were held in Paris by the cabinet and Dreyfus supporters. All parties agreed that regardless of official guilt or innocence, Dreyfus had to be freed from prison.

Mathieu Dreyfus took a train back to Rennes and after an hour convinced Alfred to withdraw his appeal and accept a pardon. A written statement was attached to the acceptance of the pardon. In it Dreyfus again stated his innocence and his determination to fight on to clear his name. On September 19, President Loubet signed the pardon decree. Ironically, Senator Scheurer-Kestner, one of Dreyfus's first important crusaders, died that morning. The next day, Alfred Dreyfus was released from prison.

Alfred and Mathieu took a train to Avignon on a roundabout route mapped out by the police as a security precaution. They stopped for a meal in a restaurant and for the first time in nearly five years Alfred found himself at a beautifully ordered table set with fine silver and china. It was clear that it would take time to readjust to the real world.

From the train station at Avignon it was a short journey by carriage to the town of Carpentras where Alfred would spend some quiet time with his family at the home of his oldest sister, Henriette, who was so close to him during his childhood. There, amid restful surroundings, he was finally reunited with his two children. "He kissed them both passionately and pressed them again and again to his heart, tears of joy coursing down his face as he did so, unable to speak."

Even as thousands of congratulatory letters and telegrams poured into Carpentras, the nationalist press in France continued its fight: "Nothing can justify the pardon"; "Dreyfus is a traitor and his pardon will not alter that fact."

In an effort to defuse matters, General de Gallifet, the minister of war, issued a special order to the army on September 21. "The incident is closed. The military judges, the object of universal respect, have delivered their verdict in complete independence. We have, without any sort of reservation, bowed down before their decree. We shall likewise bow down before the act which a sentiment of profound pity has dictated to the President of the Republic. . . . So, I repeat, the incident is closed. . . . I ask you, and if need be I should order you, to forget the past in order to think only of the future. . . ."

Georges Clemenceau, whose newspaper had originally published Zola's *J'accuse,* commented later that the pardon was inevitable. "The government had to grant it quickly to wipe out the effects of an unjust sentence. The conscience of the civilized world had risen in protest against it."

· EIGHT ·

Honor Restored

The incident is closed. —*General de Gallifet*

It is not closed. —*Alfred Dreyfus*

FOR DREYFUS, the pardon was not an end but a beginning to his renewed quest for justice. He remained in Carpentras for several months recuperating from the tremendous physical and emotional ordeal of the previous five years. To the disappointment of his supporters, he refused to be drawn into the highly charged Dreyfusard campaign for revenge against the generals and the army. But, not content with his release from prison, he wanted a complete reversal of the Rennes verdict by a legal finding of innocence and reinstatement in the army he loved.

For the government also, the pardon was only a beginning. With a deep interest in ending the entire Dreyfus Affair, Prime Minister Waldeck-Rousseau, on November 17, 1899, proposed a sweeping amnesty. In effect, the amnesty would prevent any court charges from being brought by or against anyone involved in the Dreyfus case except for Dreyfus himself. Even pending cases would be dismissed. As final preparations were made for the opening of the World's Fair in Paris, it was time to forget the past and guide France into a new century.

Not everyone was immediately in favor. Most Dreyfusards were angry. An amnesty would not allow charges to be brought against General Mercier, Major Esterhazy, or Colonel du Paty: neither could Colonel Picquart and Émile Zola pursue their legal claims. Alfred and Mathieu did not like the idea of an amnesty either but did not join in public protest against it. Picquart, in particular, was upset at this lack of support. "You are forgetting your friends," Labori admonished Mathieu.

To seek peace and quiet, Alfred took his family to Geneva, Switzerland. There, away from reporters and admirers, he enjoyed the company of his wife and children. During these first few years after his release both Alfred and Mathieu constantly searched for further evidence with which to overturn the Rennes conviction. They did not have any significant success.

It took over a year for the amnesty bill to make its way through the Senate and the Chamber of Deputies. Ironically, the newest member of the Senate, General Mercier, participated in the debate. At times, the discussion was so heated it seemed as if The Dreyfus Affair would never end, but Waldeck-Rousseau stubbornly defended his idea. "The amnesty does not judge, it does not accuse, it does not acquit: it ignores." The bill passed the Chamber of Deputies on December 24, 1900.

Dreyfus returned to Paris in December 1900, to find that many of his key supporters had fallen out with one another. It hurt him deeply to watch the disintegration of the close-knit group once so dedicated to him. But they were, after all, individuals with differing political and personal agendas whose only common connection was Dreyfus. As public interest in the Affair waned during 1900, there was less and less to keep them together. At an arranged meeting in Labori's office, an embittered

The Traitor, *by V. Lenepveu, 1900. In a series of political posters known as the "Museum of Horrors," prominent Dreyfusards were depicted as animals. Here Alfred Dreyfus is shown as a mythical Hydra.*

Colonel Picquart refused to even shake Dreyfus's hand. On his way out, in an outer room, Dreyfus wept. The world was changing.

On the night of September 29, 1902, both Émile Zola and his wife were overcome by fumes from their bedroom fireplace. The flue had somehow been blocked. While some Dreyfusards imagined something sinister, most people accepted it as merely a horrible accident. Madame Zola recovered; Émile Zola died.

Dreyfus, truly heartbroken, stood by Madame Zola at the casket and attended the funeral service. Symbolizing the change in times, a cabinet minister was present to represent the government. The eulogy was delivered by Anatole France, a leading writer and committed Dreyfusard, who concluded by saying that Zola was "for one moment, the conscience of humanity."

Meanwhile, Waldeck-Rousseau put his "republican defense" policy into practice. With The Dreyfus Affair, which had long been the rallying cause of the political Left, now closed, the prime minister could focus on other long suppressed agendas. For supporters of the French Republic it was time to flex their newly gained political muscle.

The Catholic Church, to which nearly all people in France belonged, had been largely opposed to the republican form of government. With its near total control over education in the country, its anti-republican views were kept alive from one generation to another. It was no accident that many anti-Revisionist leaders were influenced by the clergy.

Aware of the influence the clergy had upon the army, Waldeck-Rousseau set out to neutralize the power of religious organizations. In early January 1900, police searched the offices of La Croix, the newspaper of the Assumptionists, a new Catholic order. There, cash and documents were discovered which pointed to the order's involvement in anti-Revisionist activities. Within a short time the government ordered the Assumptionists to dissolve.

On July 1, 1901, the Law of Associations passed, giving the

government the right to dissolve certain religious organizations. It also made the government responsible for authorizing the establishment of each organization and monitoring its wealth.

The prime minister also took aim at army promotion practices which for years had been in the hands of monarchists, rightists, and clergy-influenced officers. A new rule now put responsibility for promotions in the hands of the new minister of war, General André. General de Gallifet had resigned in May 1900. André wasted no time in developing his own prejudiced system for only promoting officers who were republican and anti-clerical. The new "system" led to a government scandal and forced his resignation in November 1904.

In the national elections of 1902, The Dreyfus Affair was nearly forgotten. The coalition of Leftist parties, opposed to Church influence, won 339 out of 590 seats in the Chamber of Deputies. For the parties of the Right, who defended the religious organizations, difficult times were ahead. On June 3, Waldeck-Rousseau resigned and was replaced by Dr. Émile Combes, a zealous opponent of Church influence. Within a year, over fifteen thousand Catholic institutions were closed. In 1904 France broke diplomatic relations with the Vatican and severely curbed teaching by members of religious orders. On July 3, 1905, the French Parliament passed a law totally separating church and state.

Dreyfus, in retirement, kept apart from the political upheavals. He was interested in only one thing: clearing his name. But to bring a revision request of the Rennes verdict to the High Court of Appeals he needed to present some new evidence. Ever since the Rennes trial, rumors abounded about the existence of a photographic copy of an "annotated bordereau," one with the German Kaiser's handwriting. Using that alleged document as the basis for reopening debate, Jean Jaurès, a Parliament member and affirmed Dreyfusard, spoke at length in the Chamber of Deputies on April 7, 1903. With great emotion he reviewed the

Affair and the need to provide Dreyfus, at last, with the justice he deserved.

In response, General André, the minister of war, addressed the Chamber. "I believe that the conscience of the country has been disturbed to an unusual degree by the appearance of extenuating circumstances. The government is desirous of facilitating the search for the truth in this case and it would be completely amenable to an order to undertake an administrative investigation." This was the opening Dreyfus needed to reactivate his case.

For the next six months, the offices of the Statistical Section were turned upside down in a search for all documents relevant to the Dreyfus case. In the sweep, a number of Henry forgeries were found which unconditionally proved Dreyfus's innocence. Interestingly, it was Gribelin, the archivist who once aided Henry, who now devoted himself to uncovering the lies.

Among the documents uncovered were:

1. An April 1895 letter from a French secret agent containing information about a German spy who perfectly fit Esterhazy's description.
2. A letter from the Italian attaché, Panizzardi, in which the initial "P" had been changed by Henry to "D" and used to incriminate Dreyfus. This letter was cited by Cavaignac in his famous speech before the Chamber of Deputies.
3. Another letter from Panizzardi concerning details of the French railway system, cited in the bordereau. It was dated March 28, 1895, three months after the first Dreyfus trial. Henry, it was now clear, had altered the year to read "1894" to prove Dreyfus's guilt.

In October 1903, André submitted his conclusive report to the prime minister, who turned it over to the minister of justice, who in turn submitted it to a special committee. The unanimous decision was that new evidence did exist for another revision of the Dreyfus case. Finally, the appeal reached the High Court.

The legal process was slow and deliberate. The appeal passed from one court division to another. Witnesses from the previous trials were again summoned. Mercier, Gonse, du Paty, and Picquart retold their stories. Even Madame Bastian, the cleaning woman who started it all, appeared. To the embarrassment of the German government, her involvement was now public knowledge. She complained bitterly about the loss of income from her spy job.

Even Bertillon, the handwriting expert, reappeared with his strange theories. Only this time, other experts, respected scientists and academics, also testified. Their reasoned approach quickly and decisively demolished Bertillon's farfetched claims and clearly showed that only Esterhazy could have written the bordereau.

It took until July 1906 for the court to reach a decision. One stumbling block was the question of returning Dreyfus to yet another court-martial. That did not happen. It was clear that even with all the evidence now available, another military trial would not alter the 1894 and Rennes guilty verdicts.

On July 12, 1906, the judges of the United High Court of Appeals handed down their verdict. Nearly twelve years after the first conviction, Alfred Dreyfus was declared innocent of all charges against him. The Rennes verdict was overturned. At the defendant's request, there was no monetary award. Instead, the court ruled that its decision would be publicly posted in Paris and Rennes and printed in newspapers throughout the country.

Lucie, Mathieu, and the children were in the court to witness the historic moment. Alfred received the news at home. Later he told a reporter, "I am now at the end of my suffering. My honor is restored."

The next day, the Senate and the Chamber of Deputies voted overwhelmingly to reinstate Alfred Dreyfus to the army with the rank of major and named him a knight of the Legion of Honor. Colonel Picquart was also remembered. He was reinstated with the rank of brigadier general.

Several weeks later, on July 21, 1906, there was a ceremony in one of the small courtyards of the École Militaire which restored Dreyfus to his beloved army. A short distance away was the site of the degradation ceremony of 1894, the lowest point in his life. The small courtyard was chosen for this ceremony because Dreyfus did not know if he could bear the remembrance of his earlier ordeal.

As trumpets blared and a small contingent of troops came to attention, General Gillain drew his sword and touched it three times to Dreyfus's shoulder. "In the name of the President of the Republic, I make you a Knight of the Legion of Honor." He then carefully pinned the medal on the newly commissioned officer and kissed him on both cheeks.

Then, the assembled troops passed in review before the general and the major. As the officers marched by they saluted Dreyfus with their sabers. Lucie watched proudly from a window overlooking the courtyard. From another nearby window General Picquart observed the scene with equal pleasure. He had momentarily put aside his anger with Dreyfus to relish this satisfying moment.

After the ceremony, some of the small crowd of onlookers vigorously shouted, "Long live Dreyfus!"

"No," Dreyfus admonished them. "Long live France! Long live the Republic!" As he stood receiving the good wishes of other officers and friends, his son, Pierre, now fifteen years old, rushed up to embrace him. It was only then that Dreyfus betrayed his emotions: tears rolled down his cheeks.

"What a splendid day of restitution this had been for France and the Republic! My case was at an end," Dreyfus later said.

In October, exactly twelve years after his arrest, Major Alfred Dreyfus reported for duty at the Vincennes garrison. He was welcomed back warmly by fellow officers, in spite of the fact

Colonel Dreyfus (second from right) after the Ceremony of Rehabilitation at the École Militaire in 1906. He is wearing the Legion of Honor on his chest.

that some of his superiors still harbored anti-Semitic views. He was even the guest of honor at a banquet given at the Army Club by artillery officers of the First Cavalry Division.

Nonetheless, he retired from the army less than a year later. Due to the wording of the law which reinstated him, his promotion to major was without seniority thereby making him the most junior of all majors in the French army. Additional promotions would be extremely difficult. In making his formal request to retire he stipulated that he would not accept any pension due him. For him, it was payment enough to have regained his honor.

· NINE ·

The Last Survivor

My life belongs to my country: my honor does not. *—Alfred Dreyfus*

IN RETIREMENT, Dreyfus removed himself from the public eye and settled into a quiet, unhurried life surrounded by family and interests. He enjoyed reading and avidly collected every article he could find about the Affair. He also began to collect stamps, many from the letters he received from admirers around the world. He was the subject of a number of books on the Affair, and his own book, *Five Years of My Life,* written in 1901, was well received in France and, in translation, abroad.

After the years of suffering on Devil's Island his health was still very fragile. He suffered from unexplained fevers and continual fatigue. Night was the worst time. Then, wracked by nightmares, he relived the ordeals of the past. There was nothing he looked forward to as much as the yearly summer visits to Switzerland. Amidst the tranquility of lakes and mountains, Dreyfus renewed his spirits. Frequently, the vacation ended with a short stay in Italy.

On June 4, 1908, he was present as the ashes of Émile Zola were transferred to the Pantheon in Paris, the resting place of France's immortals. At the conclusion of the impressive ceremony, as the president of France departed, a nationalist writer by the name of Gregori approached Major Dreyfus and fired two shots. Miraculously, Dreyfus was only slightly wounded and recovered fully. "My blow was aimed less at Dreyfus than at Dreyfusism," the would-be assassin said. In spite of his arrest at the scene, a jury found Gregori innocent on the grounds of temporary insanity.

During the summer of 1914, as soon as he heard that France was being mobilized for an imminent war with Germany, Dreyfus returned home from a Swiss vacation. Despite lingering ailments, the stooped and frail retired major could not ignore his country's need. On August 2, he reported to the fortress at Vincennes and was assigned to an artillery depot outside Paris.

Next, at his own request, he was assigned to command the artillery of a field division and saw action in the bloody battles of Verdun and Chemin des Dames. In the midst of the fighting at Verdun, he was momentarily reunited with his son, Pierre, an officer in the same division.

In 1918, Dreyfus was promoted to lieutenant colonel and elevated to officer rank of the Legion of Honor. Then, because of his age, he was assigned to the rear and given command of an artillery depot away from the front lines. Lucie, meanwhile, busied herself as a volunteer in Paris military hospitals. When the war ended, Alfred returned again to the peace of his family-oriented home.

As he grew older, he enjoyed his expanding family. Both children married and eventually had families of their own. Alfred looked forward to the frequent visits of grandchildren. Although his physical condition weakened, he enjoyed his long daily walks. His mind was clear and active to the end.

Lieutenant Colonel Alfred Dreyfus in later life.

The Last Survivor

Colonel Alfred Dreyfus died on July 12, 1935, at the age of seventy-five, exactly twenty-nine years after he was declared innocent by the High Court. He was buried in a quiet private ceremony in the Montparnasse Jewish Cemetery two days later. In a fitting end for a man who was so dedicated to France, the date was July 14, Bastille Day, the French national holiday commemorating the Revolution of 1789.

With the death of Dreyfus all the important players in the Affair were gone.

Scheurer-Kestner was the first to go: then, Zola. Bernard Lazare, one of Dreyfus's early supporters, died in 1903 at the age of thirty-eight. Zola, whose *J'accuse* stirred the conscience of the world, died a year earlier. Jean Jaurès, who so successfully arranged the appeal of the Rennes verdict, was assassinated in 1914. Edgar Demange, the loyal attorney who defended Dreyfus twice, died in 1925 a poor and broken man. His clients had gradually deserted him because of his continued friendship with the Dreyfus family.

Georges Clemenceau ultimately became prime minister of France in 1906. In a characteristic move, he appointed Brigadier General Picquart as his minister of war. Clemenceau again assumed control of the government near the end of World War I and led France to victory. He died in 1929 without ever seeing Dreyfus again.

Georges Picquart was never totally accepted by his military colleagues because of his Dreyfusard activities. After the amnesty was declared he had nothing to do with Dreyfus and, in fact, became increasingly anti-Semitic. He assumed command of the Second Army Corps at the beginning of World War I and died on January 19, 1914, from injuries suffered in a fall from his horse. In honor of his loyalty, he received a state funeral.

Colonel du Paty de Clam, who was forced into early retirement because of his involvement in the Affair, was restored to a command position in 1912. He fought bravely and honorably during World War I and died of battle wounds in 1916.

General de Boisdeffre died a broken man in 1919. General Mercier retained his seat in the Senate until 1920, and died a year later at the age of eighty-six.

Edouard Drumont, the anti-Semitic publisher of *La Libre Parole,* died in poverty in 1917. By then, his influence had been much diminished as the vicious hatred he championed for so long fell out of fashion.

Mathieu Dreyfus, who fought so stubbornly for his brother's release, died in October 1930. Once the Rennes verdict was overturned, he returned to Mulhouse to manage the family business. He was saddened by the turn of events after Alfred was pardoned. In particular, he deplored the in-fighting among former friends who were less interested in his brother than in the cause he represented. The loss of Picquart's friendship and, for a time, Clemenceau's, greatly hurt him. The deaths of his son and son-in-law during World War I also affected him deeply.

While Alfred Dreyfus fought bravely during the war, a voice critical of France surfaced from England. The commentaries by a certain "Fitzgerald" ranted constantly against the French army. It was none other than the arch-villain of The Dreyfus Affair, Count Esterhazy. By then, no one doubted his guilt. Yet, supporters still could be found in France. Each month, a check arrived in his post office box from France which allowed him to survive. Esterhazy died a poor man in Hertfordshire, England, in 1923, where he lived under the name Count Jean de Voilemont.

Lucie Dreyfus, who stood valiantly beside her husband all their married life, died in 1945. She managed to survive World War II. Rarely did she speak of the Affair which so affected her life. Like her husband, who died ten years earlier, she was devoted to her children and grandchildren.

Pierre Dreyfus died in an airplane crash in 1946. Jeanne died in 1981.

In Germany, meanwhile, Colonel Maximilian von Schwarzkoppen left retirement during World War I to command a bri-

The Last Survivor

gadc which saw heavy action. Following recuperation from a riding accident, he was sent to the Eastern Front where he took ill and was returned to Berlin. He died on January 8, 1917. His last words concerned the Affair in which he had played a key role. "Frenchmen, hear me! Dreyfus is innocent! It was all just intrigue and forgery. Dreyfus is innocent!"

133

· TEN ·

A Country Divided

Save us. You must save the Army's
honor. —*Major Henry*

FROM 1894 through 1906—and for years beyond—The Dreyfus
Affair captured world attention. Most people found it too com-
plex to understand. An entire country was divided into factions
and laid emotionally bare as the rest of the world looked on in
disbelief. How could such injustice occur in the very land whose
revolution in 1789 gave democracy to Europe? Beginning in
1894 with Dreyfus's first court-martial, the ideals of liberty,
equality, and fraternity temporarily disappeared from the conscience of the French nation.

The Dreyfus Affair is the story of one man's terrible suffering. Some cursed him as traitor: others praised him as martyr. It
didn't matter. For within a short period of time, his individual
struggle was overshadowed by greater moral and historical is-
sues. The affair which bore his name had more to do with the

role of the military in a democracy and with the evils of anti-Semitism than it did with Alfred Dreyfus, the individual.

When asked how much Dreyfus actually understood of the Affair and all its political and religious implications, Georges Clemenceau, later to be the French prime minister, sadly answered, "Nothing. He is the only one who has not understood it at all."

Not everyone in France regarded the Revolution of 1789 with equal respect. Some, in the second half of the nineteenth century, still clinging to past glories and traditions, hoped for the restoration of the monarchy and the ordered life once symbolized by the close cooperation of the ruling classes and the clergy. By the 1890s, a fragile republican form of democracy had managed to survive attacks from monarchists, clergy, and aristocrats. After the humiliating war of 1870, in which Alsace and Lorraine were seized by Germany, the political scene became chaotic as governments rose and fell. To many, the army and the Church were the only stable institutions which continued to symbolize France's ancient greatness.

By blindly supporting the honor of the army, anti-Dreyfusards thought they were asserting the highest form of patriotism. For them, any criticism of the army, no matter how insignificant, was an affront to the entire French nation. Alfred Dreyfus's guilt or innocence was not the major issue. As one army officer said, "Although I think Dreyfus is innocent, I should still convict him for the honor of the army."

One after another, leading military officers invoked "the honor of the army" as an excuse to cover illegal activities. For many French people, preserving that "honor" exceeded the democratic principles upon which the French nation was founded.

Added to this obvious miscarriage of justice was the ease in which the Dreyfus case led to a nationwide campaign against Jews. Dreyfus was innocent. Yet, even if he were guilty, why should all French Jews be condemned for the crime of one Jew?

Alfred Dreyfus

A Country Divided

For many centuries the Jews of Europe had become a people apart: living on European soil but not considered equal to their non-Jewish neighbors. But, beginning with the French Revolution in 1789, a spirit of "enlightenment" descended upon Europe in varying degrees of intensity. For the Jews, the impossible had come true. The confining spirit of the ghetto was broken and Jews could, for the first time, dream of attaining at least limited rights of citizenship in the countries where they had lived for so long.

That breath of fresh air did not mean instant total equality. It was difficult to erase centuries of superstition and religious hatred with the stroke of a pen. But they could attend public schools and gain admission to the universities. Of perhaps greater importance was their right to equal justice, to political activity, and even to service in their country's army. Full freedom did not come to the Jews of France until 1830.

As Jews began to participate more prominently in the political, social, and business life of France, many Christians still could not accept them as equals. Among them, anti-Semitism was a "respectable" belief. Many Jews, yearning to be accepted as full and equal members of French society, dropped the strict practices of their religion. During the nineteenth century thousands went so far as to totally abandon their Judaism and convert to Christianity. But many more Jews, like the Dreyfus family, assimilated themselves into French life and did not sever their connections to Judaism.

In this climate of political upheaval, it was not difficult for the anti-Semitism of Edouard Drumont to take hold among those opposed to democracy and the Republic. With all the changes and uncertainties, people groped for normalcy. They also looked for a convenient scapegoat on whom to lay the guilt for all their political, economic, and diplomatic problems. Thus, a large segment of the French population, including aspects of the military and the Church, fell prey to the ancient hatreds many hoped had died in the revolution of 1789.

The divisive debate was fueled by a strident press. And in Paris, the center of the art world, artists took sides as well. Monet, Pissarro, and Cassat were Dreyfusard while Cézanne, Renoir, and Dégas were vehement in opposition. The large number of journalists and newspapers competed for the services of those artists whose work attracted the most readers. The artists on both sides presented the public with biting and incisive glances at all aspects of the Affair. Some, like Dégas and Toulouse-Lautrec, carried stereotyped caricatures of Jews over into later-to-be-famous nonjournalistic art. The Affair was also depicted on widely circulated postcards, posters, and board games.

For Jews, The Dreyfus Affair struck a warning bell. If they could not enjoy liberty in France, their lives in other countries were certainly in jeopardy. Theodor Herzl, the founder of political Zionism, understood this and began working tirelessly for the reestablishment of the Jewish homeland in Palestine.

The modern world was introduced to a politically "respectable" anti-Semitism: forty years later the Holocaust occurred. Interestingly, the same anti-Semitic venom found in France during The Dreyfus Affair resurfaced in Nazi Germany.

Historian Hannah Arendt saw The Dreyfus Affair as a rehearsal for Hitler's reign of terror during World War II. "What was surprising," she said, "was the organization of the mob and hero worship enjoyed by its leaders."

During World War II, as Germany occupied much of northern France, a French government under Marshal Henri Pétain, was established in Vichy in southern France with Nazi agreement. Pétain had near dictatorial power as the French Republic ended. His hope was to establish a French nation based on an authoritarian government and a strengthened clergy. Echoes of earlier anti-Semitism reverberated throughout Vichy France. Some saw Vichy as the revenge of the generals for their humiliations during The Dreyfus Affair. With the defeat of the Nazis, the Vichy government fell and Marshal Pétain was sent to prison.

A Country Divided

Supporters of the Third Republic understood that the Dreyfus case posed a danger to French democracy. For if justice were withheld from just one individual, even to preserve the "honor of the army," then no French citizen's rights were secure. Theodore Roosevelt, who was soon to be elected president of the United States, reflected on The Dreyfus Affair by saying, "It was less Dreyfus on trial than those who tried him."

It should not be forgotten that with the end of the Affair, Alfred Dreyfus did receive the justice he sought. The system did ultimately work and those who fought so bitterly to deny him his rights were decisively stopped. The power of the generals was diminished and France passed laws to strictly separate church and state. The French Republic was strengthened and its survival assured.

In France, where the anti-Semitism of The Dreyfus Affair once divided a country, a resurgence of racial and religious hatred at present targets Jews and Muslims as "outsiders." Jean-Marie LePen, leader of the right-wing National Front, has been blamed for inciting violence. In words reminiscent of the past, he loudly proclaimed, "Racism in France today means patriotism!"

In May 1990, in Carpentras, where Alfred Dreyfus went to recuperate after his release from prison, a savage anti-Semitic incident took place which shocked the civilized world. Graves at the Jewish cemetery were desecrated and a Jewish corpse mutilated. In an act of solidarity against the haters, President François Mitterrand led a quarter of a million French mourners in Paris, Jews and non-Jews, on a symbolic protest march against hatred. Throughout France, newspapers analyzed the current examples of racial and religious intolerance by referring back to The Dreyfus Affair.

The Dreyfus Affair was an important historical event which had a profound effect on the world beyond the borders of France. It taught that if injustice and religious hatred could become a way of life in a democratic country like France, it could happen anywhere.

Timeline

October 9, 1859	Alfred Dreyfus born at Mulhouse in Alsace.
1870	The Franco-Prussian War in which Alsace is annexed from France by Germany.
1880	Lieutenant Dreyfus graduates from the École Polytechnique.
April 21, 1890	Dreyfus marries Lucie Hadamard.
January 1, 1893	Dreyfus assigned to the General Staff as a probationary officer.
July 20, 1894	Major Esterhazy meets Colonel Schwarzkoppen at the German Embassy in Paris for the first time to offer his services as a spy.
August 5–12, 1894	Esterhazy attends artillery maneuvers.
September 1, 1894	Bordereau received at German Embassy.

Timeline

September 1894	Madame Bastian delivers paper scraps, including the bordereau, to French army Intelligence.
October 6, 1894	Dreyfus suspected as bordereau author.
October 15, 1894	Captain Alfred Dreyfus arrested.
October 29, 1894	*La Libre Parole* article identifies Dreyfus as traitor.
November 1, 1894	Panizzardi, the Italian military attaché, sends telegram to Rome denying any association with Dreyfus.
December 19, 1894	Secret court-martial of Captain Dreyfus begins. Concludes on December 22. Dreyfus sentenced to life deportation.
January 5, 1895	Military degradation ceremony of Captain Dreyfus at the École Militaire.
April 13, 1895	Dreyfus arrives on Devil's Island.
July 1, 1895	Major Georges Picquart becomes chief of the army Intelligence Service.
March 1896	Picquart discovers the "petit bleu."
August 1896	Picquart confirms Esterhazy as author of the bordereau.
November 1896	Picquart leaves on extended duty to North Africa.
April 2, 1987	Picquart writes addition to his will.
August 17, 1897	Esterhazy "retired" from army.
October 23, 1897	Colonel du Paty meets secretly with Esterhazy for the first time.
November 12, 1897	Dreyfus's hut surrounded by stockade fence.
November 17, 1897	General de Pellieux begins the first of his investigations of Esterhazy.
January 11, 1898	Esterhazy acquitted by court-martial.

Timeline

January 13, 1898	Zola's *J'accuse* appears. Anti-Semitic riots erupt throughout France.
February 7, 1898	Zola trial begins. Found guilty.
February 26, 1898	Picquart dismissed from army.
July 7, 1898	Cavaignac addresses Parliament.
July 16, 1898	Zola flees to England.
August 31, 1898	Colonel Henry commits suicide.
September 1, 1898	Esterhazy flees to England.
September 29, 1898	High Court begins deliberation of Dreyfus revision request.
June 3, 1899	United High Court annuls the 1894 Dreyfus conviction and orders a new trial.
June 4, 1899	Zola returns from England.
June 9, 1899	Dreyfus sails for France aboard the *Sfax*.
August 7, 1899	Rennes court-martial begins. Five weeks later Dreyfus is convicted again, but with "extenuating circumstances."
September 19, 1899	Dreyfus accepts pardon and is released from prison the next day.
November 17, 1899	Prime Minister Waldeck-Rousseau introduces amnesty bill in Parliament.
April 14, 1900	World's Fair opens in Paris.
May 1, 1901	Dreyfus's book, *Five Years of My Life*, appears.
September 29, 1902	Zola dies accidentally.
April 7, 1903	Jaurès demands revision of Rennes verdict.
July 3, 1905	Parliament passes law separating church and state.

Timeline

July 12, 1906	High Court annuls Rennes verdict without calling for a new court-martial.
July 13, 1906	Parliament votes to reinstate Dreyfus and Picquart into the army.
July 21, 1906	Dreyfus inducted into the Legion of Honor in a ceremony at the École Militaire.
July 26, 1907	Dreyfus retires from the army.
June 4, 1908	Zola's ashes transferred to the Pantheon. Dreyfus shot by would-be assassin.
August 2, 1914	Dreyfus returns to serve in French army during World War I.
May 21, 1923	Esterhazy dies in England.
July 12, 1935	Colonel Alfred Dreyfus dies in Paris.

Third Republic Personalities During The Dreyfus Affair

Year	President	Prime Minister	Minister of War
1894–1895	Casimir-Perier	Dupuy	Mercier
1895	Faure	Ribot	Mercier
1895–1896		Bourgeois	Cavaignac
1896–1898		Meline	Billot
1898		Brisson	Cavaignac
			Zurlinden
			Chanoine
1898–1899		Dupuy	Freycinet
1899	Loubet	Waldeck-Rousseau	Gallifet
			André
1902–1905		Combes	André
1905–1906		Rouvier	Berteaux
			Thomson
1906	Fallières	Sarrien	Etienne
1906–1909		Clemenceau	Picquart

Who's Who in
The Dreyfus Affair

Bastian, Marie-Caudron	The most infamous cleaning woman in France. Spy for French Intelligence at the German Embassy in Paris. (Anti-Dreyfusard)
Bertillon, Alphonse *(1853–1914)*	Noted police identification expert. Served as handwriting expert during Dreyfus trials. (Anti-Dreyfusard)
Billot, General Jean *(1828–1907)*	Minister of war, 1882–1883, 1896–1898. Ordered arrest of Picquart. (Anti-Dreyfusard)
Boisdeffre, General Raoul *(1839–1919)*	Army chief of staff, 1893–1898. (Anti-Dreyfusard)
Cavaignac, Godefroy *(1853–1905)*	Minister of war, 1895–1896, 1898. Delivered famous speech to Chamber

of Deputies quoting documents from secret file he later discovered were forgeries. Ordered Henry's arrest. (Anti-Dreyfusard)

Clemenceau, Georges
(1841–1929)

Political editor of *L'Aurore*. Published Zola's *J'accuse*. Prime Minister, 1906. (Dreyfusard)

Demange, Edgar
(1841–1925)

Lawyer for Dreyfus at both trials. (Dreyfusard)

Dreyfus, Captain Alfred
(1859–1935)

Accused of spying for Germany. Sentenced to life deportation on Devil's Island. Center of political controversy for twelve years. Innocence finally established in 1906.

Drumont, Edouard
(1844–1917)

Anti-Semitic leader. Publisher of *La Libre Parole*. (Anti-Dreyfusard)

Du Paty de Clam, Major Mercier
(1853–1916)

Officer on General Staff who investigated Dreyfus in 1894. Involved with Esterhazy to cover up illegal practices of army. (Anti-Dreyfusard)

Esterhazy, Ferdinand Walsin
(1847–1923)

Gambler. Spy. Author of the bordereau which was used to falsely imprison Dreyfus. Fled to England. (Anti-Dreyfusard)

Forzinetti, Major Ferdinand

Governor of the Cherche-Midi prison. Befriended Dreyfus. (Dreyfusard)

Gallifet, General Gaston
(1830–1909)

Minister of war, 1899–1900. Declared to army, "The incident is closed," after Dreyfus pardoned.

Gonse, General Charles
(1838–1917)

Deputy chief of staff. Involved in cover-up plotting with Major Henry, du Paty, and Esterhazy. (Anti-Dreyfusard)

Who's Who in The Dreyfus Affair

Gribelin, Felix	Archivist in Statistical Section.
Henry, Major Hubert *(1847–1898)*	On Statistical Section staff. Tampered with evidence to show Dreyfus guilty. Plotted against Major Picquart whom he succeeded as chief of Intelligence. Guilt as forger discovered. Committed suicide. (Anti-Dreyfusard)
Jaurès, Jean *(1859–1914)*	Member, Chamber of Deputies. Led fight for a court review of the Dreyfus case.
Jouaust, Colonel Albert	President of the Rennes court-martial.
Labori, Fernand *(1860–1917)*	Lawyer for Émile Zola and later, with Demange, represented Dreyfus at Rennes trial. Shot during trial. (Dreyfusard)
Lazare, Bernard *(1865–1903)*	French writer. Author of pamphlet in support of Dreyfus which helped influence public opinion. (Dreyfusard)
Leblois, Louis *(1854–1927)*	Friend of Picquart. The lawyer in whom Picquart confided what he knew of Dreyfus's innocence and Esterhazy's guilt. (Dreyfusard)
Mercier, General Auguste *(1833–1921)*	Ordered Dreyfus's arrest in 1894. Worked to preserve Dreyfus's guilty verdict. (Anti-Dreyfusard)
Picquart, Colonel Georges *(1854–1914)*	Head of the Statistical Section. Discovered "petit bleu" which allowed him to associate the bordereau with Esterhazy. Convinced of Dreyfus's innocence. Responsible for reopening case leading to Dreyfus's acquittal. Dismissed from

army in 1898 but reinstated and promoted in 1906. Minister of war, 1906–1909. (Dreyfusard)

Panizzardi, Colonel Allesandro — Italian military attaché in Paris.

Sandherr, Colonel Jean (1846–1897) — Head of Statistical Section in 1894. (Anti-Dreyfusard)

Scheurer-Kestner, Auguste (1833–1899) — Vice president of Senate. Early supporter of Dreyfus. (Dreyfusard)

Schwarzkoppen, Colonel Maximilian von (1850–1917) — German military attaché in Paris. Utilized Esterhazy as spy. Always denied that Dreyfus had anything to do with Germany.

Waldeck-Rousseau, René (1846–1904) — Prime minister of France, 1898–1900. Instituted vigorous anti-Church policies. At first, thought Dreyfus guilty. But changed his mind in time to assist Dreyfusard cause.

Zola, Émile (1840–1902) — Noted French writer and early supporter of the Dreyfus cause. His article, *J'accuse*, stirred the world with its clarion cry for justice. (Dreyfusard)

Selected Bibliography

Bredin, Jean-Denis. *The Affair, The Case of Alfred Dreyfus.* New York: George Braziller, 1986.

Chapman, Guy. *The Dreyfus Trials.* New York: Stein and Day, 1970.

Dreyfus, Alfred. *Five Years of My Life.* New York: Peebles Press, 1977.

Dreyfus, Alfred, and Dreyfus, Pierre. *The Dreyfus Case.* New Haven: Yale University Press, 1937.

Finkelstein, Norman H. *Theodor Herzl.* New York: Franklin Watts, 1987.

Halasz, Nicholas. *Captain Dreyfus, The Story of a Mass Hysteria.* New York: Simon & Schuster, 1955.

Harding, William. *Dreyfus, The Prisoner of Devil's Island.* New York: Associated Press, 1899. (OP)

Kleeblatt, Norman, ed. *The Dreyfus Affair: Art, Truth, and Justice.* Berkeley: University of California Press, 1987.

Lewis, David L. *Prisoners of Honor: The Dreyfus Affair.* New York: Morrow, 1973.

Snyder, Louis L. *The Dreyfus Case.* New Brunswick, NJ: Rutgers University Press, 1973.

Werstein, Irving. *The Franco-Prussian War.* New York: Messner, 1965.

Index